Pau

D0489916

W. H. Auden and Benjamin Britten, New York, *c.*1941

W. H. AUDEN

Paul Bunyan

The libretto of the operetta
by Benjamin Britten

With an Essay
by Donald Mitchell

faber and faber
LONDON · BOSTON

Libretto first published in 1976
by Faber Music Limited
This edition first published in 1988
by Faber and Faber Limited
3 Queen Square London WC1N 3AU
in association with Faber Music Limited

Phototypeset by Wilmaset, Birkenhead, Wirral
Printed in Great Britain by
Richard Clay Ltd, Bungay, Suffolk

British Library Cataloguing in Publication Data

Auden, W. H.
Paul Bunyan: an operetta in two acts.
1. Operas – Librettos
I. Title   2. Britten, Benjamin
782.81'2   ML50.B8685

ISBN 0–571–15260–0
ISBN 0–571–15142–6 Pbk.

Contents

Paul Bunyan, Op. 17, is published by Faber Music Limited. A complete recording of the work is available on Virgin Classics LP VCD 7907 101; CD VCD 7907 102; and Cassette VCD 7907 104.

List of Illustrations

Opera on an American legend.
Problem of putting the story of
Paul Bunyan on the stage

W. H. Auden

Most myths are poetical history – that is to say, they are not pure fantasy, but have a basis in actual events. Even in its dreams, the human mind does not create out of nothing. The anthropomorphic gods of folk-legends may, for example, in many instances, represent memories of invaders with a superior culture; these, in their turn, should a further invasion occur, may be demoted into giants and dragons. The fantastic elaborations are an expression of the psychological attitudes of men toward real events over which they have no control. Further, myths are collective creations; they cease to appear when a society has become sufficiently differentiated for its individual members to have individual conceptions of their tasks.

America is unique in being the only country to create myths after the occurrence of the industrial revolution. Because it was an undeveloped continent with an open frontier and a savage climate, conditions favourable to myth-making still existed. These were not, as in most previous civilizations primarily political, the reflection of a cultural struggle between two races (though Bunyan does fight the Indians) but geographical. In the New World the struggle between Man and Nature was again severe enough to obliterate individual differences in the face of a collective danger.

Appearing so late in history, Paul Bunyan has no magical powers; what he does is what any man could do if he were as big and as inventive; in fact, what Bunyan accomplishes as an individual is precisely what the lumbermen managed to accomplish as a team with the help of machinery. Moreover, he is like them as a character; his dreams have all the naïve swaggering optimism of the nineteenth century; he is as Victorian as New York.

Babe, the blue ox who gives him advice, remains a puzzle; I conceive of her quite arbitrarily, as a symbol of his anima, but, so far as I know, one explanation is as valid as another. Nor have I really the slightest idea why he should fail to get on with his wife, unless it signify that those who, like lumbermen, are often away from home, rarely develop the domestic virtues.

Associated with Bunyan are a number of satellite human figures, of which the most interesting are Hel Helson, his Swedish foreman, and Johnny Inkslinger, his bookkeeper. These are eternal human types: Helson, the man of brawn but no brains, invaluable as long as he has somebody to give him orders whom he trusts, but dangerous when his consciousness of lacking intelligence turns into suspicion and hatred of those who possess it; and Inkslinger, the man of speculative and critical intelligence, whose temptation is to despise those who do the manual work that makes the life of thought possible. Both of them learn a lesson in their relations with Paul Bunyan; Helson through a physical fight in which he is the loser, Inkslinger through his stomach.

In writing an operetta about Bunyan, three difficulties arose. In the first place, his size and general mythical characteristics prevent his physical appearance on the stage – he is presented as a voice and, in order to differentiate him from the human characters, as a speaking role. In consequence someone else had to be found to play the chief dramatic role, and Inkslinger seemed the most suitable, as satisfying Henry James's plea for a fine lucid intelligence as a compositional centre. Inkslinger, in fact, is the only person capable of understanding who Paul Bunyan really is, and, in a sense, the operetta is an account of his process of discovery.

In the second place, the theatrical presentation of the

majority of Bunyan's exploits would require the resources of Bayreuth, but not to refer to them at all would leave his character all too vaguely in the air. To get round this difficulty we have interposed simple narrative ballads between the scenes, as it were, as solo Greek chorus.

Lastly, an opera with no female voices would be hard to produce and harder to listen to, yet in its earlier stages at least the conversion of forests into lumber is an exclusively male occupation. Accordingly we have introduced a camp dog and two camp cats, sung by a coloratura soprano and two mezzo-sopranos respectively.

The principal interest of the Bunyan legend today is as a reflection of the cultural problems that occur during the first stage of every civilization, the stage of colonization of the land and the conquest of nature. The operetta, therefore, begins with a prologue in which America is still a virgin forest and Paul Bunyan has not yet been born, and ends with a Christmas party at which he bids farewell to his men because now he is no longer needed. External physical nature has been mastered, and for this very reason can no longer dictate to men what they should do. Now their task is one of their human relations with each other and, for this, a collective mythical figure is no use, because the requirements of each relation are unique. Faith is essentially invisible.

At first sight it may seem presumptuous for a foreigner to take an American folk-tale as his subject, but in fact the implications of the Bunyan legend are not only American but universal.

Until the advent of the machine the conquest of nature was still incomplete, and as users of the machine all countries share a common history. All countries are now faced at the same and for the first time with the same problem. Now that, in a material sense, we can do anything almost that we like, how are we to know what is the right thing to do and what is the wrong thing to avoid, for nature is no longer a nurse with her swift punishments and rewards? Of what happens when men refuse to accept this necessity of choosing, and are terrified of or careless about their freedom, we have now only too clear a proof.

This article appeared in the *New York Times*, 4 May 1941, section 9, page 7, © 1941 by The New York Times Company. Reprinted by permission.

THE COLUMBIA THEATER ASSOCIATES PRESENT

PAUL BUNYAN

A NEW OPERETTA
IN 2 ACTS

Book by
W. H. AUDEN

Music by
BENJAMIN BRITTEN

THE WEEK OF MAY 5
BRANDER MATTHEWS HALL
420 WEST 117th STREET

EVENINGS AT 8:40 - - - SATURDAY MATINEE AT 2:40
ADMISSION 50¢ OR BY SUBSCRIPTION
BOX OFFICE OPEN DAILY FROM 10 A.M. TO 6 P.M.

The poster for the first production

PAUL BUNYAN

———

AN OPERETTA IN TWO ACTS
AND A PROLOGUE

Libretto by W. H. Auden

Set to music by Benjamin Britten
Op. 17

The first performance of *Paul Bunyan* was given by the Columbia Theater Associates of Columbia University, New York, with the co-operation of the Columbia University Department of Music and a Chorus from the New York Schola Cantorum, conducted by Hugh Ross, in Brander Matthews Hall on 5 May 1941.

Characters

(In the Prologue)
CHORUS of OLD TREES
(SATB)
FOUR YOUNG TREES
2 Sopranos, 2 Tenors
THREE WILD GEESE
2 Mezzo-sopranos,
Soprano

NARRATOR
Baritone or Tenor
(In the Ballad Interludes)

The Voice of PAUL BUNYAN
Spoken part

JOHNNY INKSLINGER
(bookkeeper)
Tenor

TINY
(daughter of Paul Bunyan)
Soprano

HOT BISCUIT SLIM
(a good cook)
Tenor

SAM SHARKEY
Tenor
BEN BENNY
Bass

(two bad cooks)

HEL HELSON
(foreman)
Baritone

ANDY ANDERSON
Tenor
PETE PETERSON
Tenor
JEN JENSON
Bass
CROSS CROSSHAULSON
Bass
(four Swedes)

JOHN SHEARS
(a farmer)
Baritone

WESTERN UNION BOY
Tenor

9

FIDO
(*a dog*)
High soprano

MOPPET
Mezzo-soprano
POPPET
Mezzo-soprano
(*two cats*)

QUARTET OF THE DEFEATED
Alto, Tenor, Baritone, Bass

FOUR CRONIES of HEL
HELSON
Four Baritones

HERON, MOON, WIND,
BEETLE, SQUIRREL
Spoken parts

Chorus of LUMBERJACKS,
FARMERS and
FRONTIER WOMEN

No. 1 Introduction

No. 2 Prologue
In the forest.

CHORUS of OLD TREES

Since the birth
Of the earth
Time has gone
On and on:
Rivers saunter,
Rivers run,
Till they enter
The enormous level sea,
Where they prefer to be.

But the sun
Is too hot,
And will not
Let alone
Waves glad-handed,
Lazy crowd,
Educates them
Till they change into a cloud,
But can't control them long.

For the will
Just to fall
Is too strong
In them all;
Revolution
Turns to rain

13

Whence more solid
Sensible Creatures gain:
In falling they serve life.

Here are we
Flower and tree,
Green, alive,
Glad to be,
And our proper
Places know:
Winds and waters
Travel; we remain and grow;
We like life to be slow.

FOUR YOUNG TREES
No. No. No. No.

CHORUS of OLD TREES
O.

FOUR YOUNG TREES
We do *Not* want life to be slow.

CHORUS of OLD TREES
Reds.

FOUR YOUNG TREES
We are *bored* with standing still,
We want to see things and go places.

CHORUS of OLD TREES
Such nonsense. It's only a phase.
They're sick. They're crazy.

(*Enter* TWO WILD GEESE.)

Ooh!
O how terrible to be
As old-fashioned as a tree:
Dull old stick that won't go out;
What on earth do they talk about?
  Unexpressive,
  Unprogressive,
Unsophisticated lout.
How can pines or grass or sage
Understand the Modern Age?

(*Enter* THIRD WILD GOOSE.)

  Ooh!
What's up, eh? Do tell us, quick!

    THREE WILD GEESE
That's the best I ever heard!
Shall we tell them? Now?
You are all to leave here.

    CHORUS of OLD TREES
What?
It's a lie!

    FOUR YOUNG TREES
Hurrah!

    CHORUS of OLD TREES
Don't listen!

    FOUR YOUNG TREES
How?

THREE WILD GEESE
Far away from here
A mission will find a performer.

CHORUS of OLD TREES
A mission?
What mission?

THREE WILD GEESE
To bring you to another life.

FOUR YOUNG TREES
What kind of performer?

THREE WILD GEESE
A Man.

FOUR YOUNG TREES
What is a man?

CHORUS of OLD TREES
What is a man?

THREE WILD GEESE
A man is a form of life
That dreams in order to act
And acts in order to dream
And has a name of his own.

FOUR YOUNG TREES and CHORUS of OLD TREES
What is this name?

THREE WILD GEESE
Paul Bunyan.

CHORUS of OLD TREES
How silly.

FOUR YOUNG TREES
When are we to see him?

THREE WILD GEESE
He will be born at the next Blue Moon.

CHORUS of OLD TREES
It isn't true,
I'm so frightened.
Don't worry.
There won't be a Blue Moon in our lifetime.
Don't say that. It's unlucky.

(The moon begins to turn blue.)

FOUR YOUNG TREES
Look at the moon! It's turning blue.

CHORUS of OLD TREES
Look at the moon! It's turning blue.

THREE WILD GEESE
It isn't very often the conservatives are wrong,
Tomorrow normally is only yesterday again,
Society is right in saying nine times out of ten
Respectability's enough to carry one along.

CHORUS of OLD TREES
But once in a while the odd thing happens,
    Once in a while the dream comes true,
And the whole pattern of life is altered,
    Once in a while the moon turns blue.

17

SEMI-CHORUS of OLD TREES

We can't pretend we like it, that it's what we'd
   choose,
But what's the point in fussing when one can't refuse
And nothing is as bad as one thinks it will be,
The children look so happy – Well, well, we shall see.

FOUR YOUNG TREES

I want to be a vessel sailing on the sea,
I want to be a roof with houses under me,
I've always longed for edges, and I'd love to be a
   square.
How swell to be a dado and how swell to be a chair.

TUTTI

But once in a while the odd thing happens,
   Once in a while the dream comes true,
And the whole pattern of life is altered,
   Once in a while the moon turns blue.

No. 2a First Ballad Interlude

NARRATOR

The cold wind blew through the crooked thorn,
Up in the North a boy was born.

His hair was black, his eyes were blue,
His mouth turned up at the corners too.

A fairy stood beside his bed;
'You shall never, never grow old,' she said,

'Paul Bunyan is to be your name';
Then she departed whence she came.

You must believe me when I say,
He grew six inches every day.

You must believe me when I speak,
He gained three–four–six pounds every week.

He grew so fast, by the time he was eight,
He was as tall as the Empire State.

The length of his stride's a historical fact;
Three point seven miles to be exact.

When he ordered a jacket, the New England mills
For months had no more unemployment ills.

When he wanted a snapshot to send to his friends,
They found they had to use a telephoto lens.

But let me tell you in advance,
His dreams were of greater significance.

His favourite dream was of felling trees,
A fancy which grew by swift degrees.

One night he dreamt he was to be
The greatest logger in history.

He woke to feel something stroking his brow,
And found it was the tongue of an enormous cow.

From horn to horn or from lug to lug,
Was forty-seven axe-heads and a baccy plug.

But what would have most bewildered you
Was the colour of her hide which was bright bright
   blue.

But Bunyan wasn't surprised at all;
Said, 'I'll call you Babe, you call me Paul.'

He pointed to a meadow, said, 'Take a bite:
For you're leaving with me for the South tonight.'

Over the mountains, across the streams
They went to find Paul Bunyan's dreams.

The bear and the beaver waved a paw,
The magpie chattered, the squirrel swore.

The trappers ran out from their lonely huts
Scratching their heads with their rifle butts.

For a year and a day they travelled fast.
'This is the place,' Paul said at last.

The forest stretched for miles around,
The sound of their breathing was the only sound.

Paul picked a pine-tree and scratched his shins,
Said, 'This is the place where our work begins.'

ACT ONE

Scene 1
A clearing in the forest.

No. 3 Bunyan's Greeting

VOICE of PAUL BUNYAN

It is a spring morning without benefit of young persons.

It is a sky that has never registered weeping or rebellion.

It is a forest full of innocent beasts. There are none who
blush at the memory of an ancient folly, none who hide
beneath dyed fabrics a malicious heart.

It is America, but not yet.

Wanted. Disturbers of public order, men without foresight
or fear.

Wanted. Energetic madmen. Those who have thought
themselves a body large enough to devour their
dreams.

Wanted. The lost. Those indestructibles whom defeat can
never change. Poets of the bottle, clergymen of a
ridiculous gospel, actors who should have been
engineers and lawyers who should have been sea-
captains, saints of circumstance, desperados,
unsuccessful wanderers, all who can hear the invitation
of the earth, America, youngest of her daughters,
awaits the barbarians of marriage.

No. 3a Call of Lumberjacks

CHORUS of LUMBERJACKS
(Starting offstage and gradually approaching)

Down the Line. Timber–rrr.

No. 4 Lumberjacks' Chorus

LUMBERJACK 1

My birthplace was in Sweden, it's a very long way
off,
My appetite was hearty but I couldn't get enough;
When suddenly I heard a roar across the wide blue
sea,
'I'll give you steak and onions if you'll come and
work for me.'

CHORUS of LUMBERJACKS

We rise at dawn of day,
We're handsome, free and gay,
   We're lumberjacks
   With saw and axe
Who are melting the forests away.

LUMBERJACK 2

In France I wooed a maiden with an alabaster skin,
But she left me for a fancy chap who played the
violin;
When just about to drown myself a voice came
from the sky,
'There's no one like a shanty boy to catch a
maiden's eye.'

CHORUS of LUMBERJACKS

We rise at dawn, etc.

LUMBERJACK 3

Oh, long ago in Germany when sitting at my ease,
There came a knocking at the door and it was the
police;
I tiptoed down the backstairs and a voice to me did
say,

'There's freedom in the forests out in North
    Americay.'

CHORUS of LUMBERJACKS
We rise at dawn, etc.

LUMBERJACK 4
In Piccadilly Circus I stood waiting for a bus,
I thought I heard the pigeons say, 'Please run away
    with us';
To a land of opportunity with work and food for
    all,
Especially for shanty boys in Winter and in Fall.

CHORUS of LUMBERJACKS
We rise at dawn, etc.

No. 4a Bunyan's Welcome

VOICE of PAUL BUNYAN:
Welcome and sit down, we have no time to waste.
The trees are waiting for the axe and we must all make
    haste.
So who shall be the foreman to set in hand the work
To organize the logging and see men do not shirk?

No. 5 Quartet of Swedes

FOUR SWEDES
    I.
      I.
        I.
          I.

CHORUS of LUMBERJACKS: Why?

FOUR SWEDES

Swedish born and Swedish bred,
Strong in the arm and dull in the head.
Who can ever kill a Swede?
His skull is very thick indeed,
But once you get an idea in,
You'll never get it out again.

VOICE of PAUL BUNYAN: What are your names?

FOUR SWEDES

Cross Crosshaulson.
Jen Jenson.
Pete Peterson.
Andy Anderson.

VOICE of PAUL BUNYAN:
In your opinion which of you, which one would be the best
To be the leader of the few and govern all the rest?

FOUR SWEDES

(*Fighting*)

Why?
Who?
You?
Oh!
No, me!
Oh, he!
Yah!
Bah!

VOICE of PAUL BUNYAN: None of you, it seems, will do.
We must find another.
CHORUS of LUMBERJACKS: Yes, but who?

(*Enter a* WESTERN UNION BOY, *on a bicycle.*)

No. 6 *Western Union Boy's Song*

WESTERN UNION BOY

A telegram, a telegram,
    A telegram from oversea.
Paul Bunyan is the name
    Of the addressee.

(*Exit across stage.*)

CHORUS of LUMBERJACKS: Bad News? Good News? Tell us
    what you're reading.
VOICE of PAUL BUNYAN: I have a message that will please
    you from the King of Sweden.
    (*Reads:*) Dear Paul,
    I hear you are looking for a head-foreman, so I'm
    sending you the finest logger in my kingdom, Hel
    Helson. He doesn't talk much. Wishing you every
    success.
        Yours sincerely,
        Nel Nelson. King.

(*Enter while he is reading* HEL HELSON.)

    Are you Hel Helson?
HEL HELSON: Aye tank so.
VOICE of PAUL BUNYAN: Do you know all about logging?
HEL HELSON: Aye tank so.
VOICE of PAUL BUNYAN: Are you prepared to be my head-
    foreman?
HEL HELSON: Aye tank so.
VOICE of PAUL BUNYAN: Then I think so too.
Now for one to cook or bake
Flapjacks, cookies, fish, or steak.

(*Enter* SAM SHARKEY *and* BEN BENNY.)

SAM SHARKEY: Sam Sharkey at your service.
BEN BENNY: Ben Benny at your service.

No. 7 Cooks' Duet

SAM SHARKEY
Sam for soups.

BEN BENNY
Ben for beans.

SAM SHARKEY
Soups feed you.

BEN BENNY
Beans for vitamins.

SAM SHARKEY
Soups satisfy,
Soups gratify.

BEN BENNY
Ten beans a day
Cure food delay.

SAM SHARKEY
Soups that nourish,
Make hope flourish,

BEN BENNY
Beans for nutrition,
Beans for ambition,

SAM SHARKEY

The Best People are crazy about soups!

BEN BENNY

Beans are all the rage among the Higher Income
    Groups!

SAM SHARKEY

Do you feel a left-out at parties,
when it comes to promotion are you passed over,
and does your wife talk in her sleep?
Then ask our nearest agent
to tell you about soups for success!

BEN BENNY

You owe it to yourself to learn about Beans, and
how this delicious food is the sure way to the Body
Beautiful.
We will mail you a fascinating booklet
'Beans for Beauty' by return of post
if you'll send us your address.

(*Enter* JOHNNY INKSLINGER.)

INKSLINGER: Did I hear anyone say something about food?
SAM SHARKEY: What about a delicious bowl of soup?
BEN BENNY: What would you say to a nice big plate of
    beans?
INKSLINGER: I'll have a double portion of both, please.

(*Exeunt* SAM SHARKEY *and* BEN BENNY.)

VOICE of PAUL BUNYAN: Good-day stranger. What's your
    name?
INKSLINGER: Johnny Inkslinger.
VOICE of PAUL BUNYAN: Can you read?
INKSLINGER: Think of a language and I'll write you its
    dictionary.

VOICE of PAUL BUNYAN: Can you handle figures?
INKSLINGER: Think of an irrational number and I'll double
    it.
VOICE of PAUL BUNYAN:
You're just the man I hoped to find
For I have large accounts to mind.
INKSLINGER: Sorry I'm busy.
VOICE of PAUL BUNYAN: What's your job?
INKSLINGER: Oh, just looking around.
VOICE of PAUL BUNYAN: Who do you work for?
INKSLINGER: Myself, silly. This is a free country.

(COOKS *enter*.)

    Excuse me.
SAM SHARKEY: Your soup.
BEN BENNY: Your beans.
BOTH: Just taste them.
VOICE of PAUL BUNYAN: Wait a minute.

(COOKS *stand back*.)

    Have you any money?
INKSLINGER: Search me.
VOICE of PAUL BUNYAN: How are you going to pay for
    your supper?
INKSLINGER: Dunno. Never thought of it.
VOICE of PAUL BUNYAN:
If you work for me
You shall eat splendidly
But no work, no pay.
INKSLINGER: No sale. Good-day.

(*Exit* INKSLINGER.)

CHORUS of LUMBERJACKS
Now what on earth are we to do
For I can't keep accounts, can you?

VOICE of PAUL BUNYAN:
Don't worry, he'll come back,
He has to feed.
Now what else do we lack,
Who else do we need?
SAM SHARKEY
I'd like a dog to lick up all the crumbs
And chase away the salesmen and all the drunken bums.
BEN BENNY
I'd like a pair of cats
To catch the mice and rats.

(PAUL BUNYAN *whistles* – *enter* FIDO, MOPPET *and* POPPET.)

No. 8 Animal Trio

FIDO

Ah!

MOPPET and POPPET

Miaou!

FIDO

The single creature lives a partial life,
Man by his eye and by his nose the hound;
He needs the deep emotions I can give,
Through him I sense a vaster hunting-ground.

MOPPET and POPPET

Like draws to like, to share is to relieve,
And sympathy the root bears love the flower;
He feels in us, and we in him perceive
A common passion for the lonely hour.

29

FIDO
In all his walks I follow at his side,
His faithful servant and his loving shade;

MOPPET and POPPET
We move in our apartness and our pride
About the decent dwellings he has made.

No. 8a Bunyan's Goodnight (i)

VOICE of PAUL BUNYAN:
Off to supper and to bed,
For all our future lies ahead,
And our work must be begun
At the rising of the sun.

(*Exeunt.*)

No. 8b Exit of Lumberjacks

CHORUS of LUMBERJACKS
Down the line. Timber–rr.

No. 9 The Blues: Quartet of Defeated

VOICE of PAUL BUNYAN:
Now at the beginning
To those who pause on the frontiers of an untravelled
    empire
Standing in empty dusk upon the eve of a tremendous task,
    to you all
A dream of warning.

TENOR SOLO
Gold in the North came the blizzard to say,
I left my sweetheart at the break of day,
The gold ran out and my love grew grey.
    You don't know all, sir, you don't know all.

BASS SOLO
The West, said the sun, for enterprise,
A bullet in Frisco put me wise,
My last words were, 'God damn your eyes!'
　　You don't know all, sir, you don't know all.

ALTO SOLO
In Alabama my heart was full,
Down to the river bank I stole,
The waters of grief went over my soul.
　　You don't know all, sir, you don't know all.

BARITONE SOLO
In the streets of New York I was young and well,
I rode the market, the market fell,
One morning I found myself in hell.
　　I didn't know all, sir, I didn't know all.

ALL
　　We didn't know all, sir, we didn't know all.

BARITONE SOLO
In the saloons I heaved a sigh.

TENOR SOLO
Lost in deserts of alkali I lay down to die.

ALTO SOLO
There's always a sorrow can get you down.

BASS SOLO
All the world's whiskey can never drown.

ALL
　　You don't know all, sir, you don't know all.

Some think they're strong, some think they're
  smart,
Like butterflies they're pulled apart,

ALL
America can break your heart.
    You don't know all, sir, you don't know all.

(*Enter* INKSLINGER.)

VOICE OF PAUL BUNYAN: Hello Mr Inkslinger. Lost
  anything?
INKSLINGER: I want my supper.
VOICE OF PAUL BUNYAN: What about my little proposition?
INKSLINGER: You win. I'll take it. Now where's the kitchen,
  Mr Bunyan?
VOICE OF PAUL BUNYAN: Call me Paul.
INKSLINGER: No. You're stronger than I, so I must do what
  you ask. But I'm not going to pretend to like you. Good
  night.

(*Exit* INKSLINGER.)

No. 10 Bunyan's Goodnight (ii)

VOICE OF PAUL BUNYAN:
Good night, Johnny, and good luck.

No. 10a Second Ballad Interlude

NARRATOR
The Spring came and the Summer and Fall;
Paul Bunyan sat in his binnacle.

Regarding like a lighthouse lamp
The work going on in the lumber camps.

Dreaming dreams which now and then
He liked to tell to his lumbermen.

His phrases rolled like waves on a beach
And during the course of a single speech

Young boys grew up and needed a shave,
Old men got worried they'd be late for the grave.

He woke one morning feeling unwell,
Said to Babe: 'What's the matter? I feel like Hell.'

Babe cocked her head, said: 'Get a wife;
One can have too much of the bachelor life.'

And so one morning in the month of May
Paul went wife-hunting at the break of day.

He kept a sharp look-out, but all
The girls he saw were much too small.

But at last he came to a valley green
With mountains beside and a river between,

And there on the bank before his eyes
He beheld a girl of the proper size.

The average man if he walked in haste
Would have taken a week to get round her waist.

When you looked at her bosom you couldn't fail
To see it was built on a generous scale.

They eyed each other for an interval;
Then she said, 'I'm Carrie' and he said, 'I'm Paul.'

What happened then I've no idea,
They never told me and I wasn't there.

But whatever it was she became his wife
And they started in on the married life.

And in a year a daughter came,
Tiny she was and Tiny her name.

I wish I could say that Carrie and Paul
Were a happy pair but they weren't at all.

It's not the business of a song
To say who was right and who was wrong.

Both said the bitter things that pain
And wished they hadn't but said them again.

Till Carrie said at last one day:
'It's no use, Paul, I must go away.'

Paul struck a match and lit his pipe,
Said: 'It seems a pity but perhaps you're right.'

So Carrie returned to her home land,
Leading Tiny by the hand,

And Paul stayed in camp with his lumbermen,
Though he paid them visits now and then.

One day Tiny telegraphed him: 'Come quick.
Very worried. Mother sick.'

But the doctor met him at the door and said:
'I've bad news for you, Paul; she's dead.'

He ran upstairs and stood by the bed:
'Poor Carrie,' he murmured and stroked her head.

'I know we fought and I was to blame
But I loved you greatly all the same.'

He picked up Tiny and stroked her hair,
Said: 'I've not been much of a father, dear.

'But I'll try to be better until the day
When you want to give your heart away.

'And whoever the lucky man may be,
I hope he's a better man than me.'

So they got ready to return
To the camp, of which you now shall learn.

Scene 2
The camp.

LUMBERJACK 1: Nothing but soups and beans.
LUMBERJACK 2: Mondays, Wednesdays and Fridays soup.
LUMBERJACK 3: Tuesdays, Thursdays and Saturdays beans.
LUMBERJACK 1: Sundays, soup *and* beans.
LUMBERJACK 2: Soup gives me ulcers.
LUMBERJACK 3: I'm allergic to beans.
LUMBERJACK 1: Have you seen the chief about it, Johnny?
INKSLINGER: He's not back yet from his wife's funeral.
LUMBERJACK 2: Well, something's gotta be done about it,
    and done quick.
LUMBERJACK 3: You'll have to speak to them, yourself.
CHORUS of LUMBERJACKS: Things have gone too far.

No. 11 Food Chorus

Do I look the sort of fellow
Whom you might expect to bellow
    For a quail in aspic, or
Who would look as glum as Gandhi
If he wasn't offered brandy
    With a Lobster Thermidor?

Who would howl like some lost sinner
For a sherry before dinner,
    And demand a savoury;
Who would criticize the stuffing
In the olives, and drink nothing
    But Lapsang Suchong tea?

No, no, no, no.
Our digestion's pretty tough
And we're not particular,
But when they hand us out to eat
A lump of sandstone as the sweet,
Then things have gone too far.

Oh, the soup looks appetizing
Till you see a maggot rising
    White as Venus from the sea;
And a beetle in the cauli-
Flower isn't very jolly
    Or so it appears to me;

Flies have interesting features
And, of course they're all God's creatures,
    But a trifle out of place
In a glass of drinking water,
And it makes my temper shorter
    If I meet one face to face.

No, no, no, no.
Our digestion's pretty tough
And we're not particular,
But when we're even asked to crunch
A rat or cockroach with our lunch,
Then things have gone too far.

INKSLINGER

Iron, they say, is healthy,
And even wood is wealthy
    In essential vitamins;
But I hate to find a mallet
Tucked away in the fruit salad
    Or a hammer in the greens.

There are foods, so doctors tell you,
With a high nutritious value
    That the Middle Ages never knew;
But I can't secrete saliva
At the thought of a screwdriver
    Or a roasted walking shoe.

CHORUS of LUMBERJACKS

Our digestion's pretty tough
And we're not particular,
But when the kitchen offers one
A rusty thumb-tack underdone,
Then things have gone too far!

(*Enter* SAM SHARKEY *and* BEN BENNY.)

SAM SHARKEY and BEN BENNY: Anything wrong?
INKSLINGER: Please don't think for a moment we want to
    criticize. Your cooking's wonderful. We all know that
    Sam's soups are the finest in the world, and as for
    Ben's beans, why there isn't a dish like them anywhere.

But don't you think that just occasionally, say once a month, we could have something different?

SAM SHARKEY: I can't believe it.

BEN BENNY: It's not possible.

SAM SHARKEY and BEN BENNY: After all we've done for them.

SAM SHARKEY: Haven't you stayed awake all night thinking how to please them?

BEN BENNY: Haven't you worked your fingers to the bone?

SAM SHARKEY: Day in, day out.

BEN BENNY: Week after week, month after month.

SAM SHARKEY: Year after year.

BEN BENNY: Not a word of thanks.

SAM SHARKEY: Just grumble, grumble, grumble.

BEN BENNY: Treating us like dogs.

SAM SHARKEY: I can't bear it any longer.

BEN BENNY: You don't know how much you've hurt us.

SAM SHARKEY: My nerves.

BEN BENNY: My art.

SAM SHARKEY and BEN BENNY: Very well. Very well. From now on you shall do the cooking yourselves.

INKSLINGER: Oh, but please. We didn't mean to upset you.

SAM SHARKEY: It's all right. We understand perfectly.

INKSLINGER: Sam. Ben. Please listen. I'm sorry if . . .

BEN BENNY: Don't apologize. We're not angry.

SAM SHARKEY: Just a little sad, that's all.

BEN BENNY: One day perhaps you'll realize what you've done. Come, Sam.

SAM SHARKEY: Come, Ben.

(*Exeunt.*)

No. 12 *Chorus Accusation*

CROSS CROSSHAULSON
There now look what you have done.

INKSLINGER
What I did, you asked me to.

JEN JENSON
You know I only spoke in fun.

PETE PETERSON
I never understood what you
Meant to do.

ANDY ANDERSON
I said it wouldn't do,
You heard me, didn't you?

INKSLINGER
What would you have done instead?

CHORUS of LUMBERJACKS
Never mind. Beyond a doubt
You have put us in the red,
So you'd better get us out.

No. 12a Slim's Song

SLIM

(*Offstage*)
In fair days and in foul
    Round the world and back,
I must hunt my shadow
    And the self I lack.

(SLIM *rides on.*)

INKSLINGER: Hullo, stranger. What's your name?

SLIM: Slim.

INKSLINGER: You don't look like a logger. Where do you
come from?

SLIM

I come from open spaces
 Where over endless grass
The stroking winds and shadows
 Of cloud and bison pass;
My brothers were the buffalo,
 My house the shining day,
I danced between the horse-hoofs like
 A butterfly at play.

In fair days and in foul, etc.

One winter evening as I sat
 By my camp fire alone,
I heard a whisper from the flame,
 The voice was like my own:
'Oh get you up and get you gone,
 North, South, or East or West,
This emptiness cannot answer
 The heart in your breast.

'O ride till woods or houses
 Provide the narrow place
Where you can force your fate to turn
 And meet you face to face.'

In fair days and in foul
 Round the world and back,
I must hunt my shadow
 And the self I lack.
  FIDO, MOPPET and POPPET
Ah!

40

INKSLINGER: Say, you can't cook by any chance?
SLIM: Sure.
CHORUS of LUMBERJACKS: Can you cook flapjacks?
SLIM: Yes.
CHORUS of LUMBERJACKS: Cookies?
SLIM: Yes.
CHORUS of LUMBERJACKS: Fish?
SLIM: Yes.
CHORUS of LUMBERJACKS: Steaks?
SLIM: Yes.
CHORUS of LUMBERJACKS: Are you telling lies?
SLIM: Yes. No. No. No.
CHORUS of LUMBERJACKS
You're an angel in disguise.
Sam and Benny get the sack.

No. 13 Bunyan's Return

CHORUS of LUMBERJACKS
Look, look the Chief is back.
And look, can I believe my eyes,
Is that a girl he's got with him?
Gosh, she's pretty and young and trim.
O boy.

(*Exeunt all but* FIDO *and* INKSLINGER.)

INKSLINGER: Hello, Fido. Staying to keep me company?
That's mighty nice of you. Say, Fido, I want to ask you
a question. Are you happy?

(FIDO *shakes his head.* INKSLINGER *goes to the door and looks to see
if anyone is listening.*)
Then I'll tell you a secret. Neither am I, May I tell you
the story of my life?

41

(FIDO *nods*.)

You're sure it won't bore you?

(FIDO *shakes his head but when* INKSLINGER *is not looking stifles a yawn with a paw*.)

No. 14 Inkslinger's Song

INKSLINGER
It was out in the sticks that the fire
    Of my existence began,
Where no one had heard the *Messiah*
    And no one had seen a Cézanne.
I learned a prose style from the preacher
    And the facts of life from the hens,
And fell in love with the teacher
    Whose love for John Keats was intense.
And I dreamed of writing a novel
    With which Tolstoy couldn't compete
And of how all the critics would grovel:
    But I guess that a guy gotta eat.

I can think of much nicer professions
    Than keeping a ledger correct,
Such as writing my private confessions
    Or procuring a frog to dissect.
Learning Sanskrit would be more amusing
    Or studying the history of Spain.
And, had I the power of choosing,
    I would live on the banks of the Seine.
I would paint St Sebastian the Martyr,
    Or dig up the Temples of Crete,
Or compose a D major Sonata:
    But I guess that a guy gotta eat.

The company I have to speak to
    Are wonderful men in their way,
But the things that delight me are Greek to
    The Jacks who haul lumber all day.
It isn't because I don't love them
    That this camp is a prison to me,
Nor do I think I'm above them
    In loathing the sight of a tree.
Oh, but where are those beautiful places
    Where what you begin you complete,
Where the joy shines out of men's faces,
    And all get sufficient to eat?

No. 14a Entrance of Chorus

PETE PETERSON
I never knew he had a daughter.
ANDY ANDERSON
She's much lovelier than I thought her.
JEN JENSON
Tiny, what a pretty name.
CROSS CROSSHAULSON
I am delighted that she came.
PETE PETERSON
Her eyes,
JEN JENSON
    Her cheeks,
CROSS CROSSHAULSON
        Her lips,
ANDY ANDERSON
            Her nose.
JEN JENSON
She's a peach,
JOHN SHEARS
    A dove,

PETE PETERSON
A rose.

(*Enter* TINY.)

No. 15 Tiny's Entrance

BEN BENNY: Look at me, Miss Tiny: I'm six feet tall.

SAM SHARKEY: Look at me, Miss Tiny: I've the bluest eyes you ever saw.

CROSS CROSSHAULSON: Feel my biceps, Miss Tiny.

ANDY ANDERSON: I can ride a bicycle.

JOHN SHEARS: I can spell parallelogram.

ANDY ANDERSON: I've got fifty dollars salted away in an old sock.

JOHN SHEARS: I'll run errands for you.

SAM SHARKEY: I'll bring your breakfast in bed.

BEN BENNY: I'll tell you stories before you go to sleep.

ANDY ANDERSON: I'll make you laugh by pulling faces.

BEN BENNY: I'm big and husky. You need someone to look after you.

JOHN SHEARS: You need someone to look after; I'm sick.

No. 15a Tiny's Song

TINY

Ah!

INKSLINGER: Leave her alone, you fools. Have you forgotten her mother's just died?

TINY

Ah!
Whether the sun shines upon children playing,
Or storms endanger the sailors at sea,

44

In a solitude or a conversation,
Mother, O Mother, tears arise in me.

For underground now you rest who at nightfall
Would sing me to sleep in my little bed;
I turn with the world but grief has no motion;
Mother, O Mother, too soon you were dead.

O never again in fatigue or fever
Shall I feel your cool hand upon my brow;
As you look after the cherubs in Heaven,
Mother, O Mother, look down on me now.

Should a day come I hear a lover whisper,
Should I stay an old maid whom the men pass by,
My heart shall cherish your guardian image,
Mother, O Mother, till the day I die.

CHORUS of LUMBERJACKS
The white bone
Lies alone
Like the limestone
Under the green grass.
All time goes by;
We too shall lie
Under death's eye.
Alas, alas.

TINY

Alas.

(*Enter* SLIM.)

SLIM: Supper's ready.
TINY: Excuse me, are you the cook?

45

SLIM: Yes, mam.

TINY: I'm Miss Tiny. Father said I was to help you in the kitchen.

SLIM: I'm sure you'll be a great help, Miss Tiny. This way, please.

(*As they exeunt:*)

LUMBERJACK 1: Did you see how he looked at her?

LUMBERJACK 2: Did you see how she looked at him?

LUMBERJACK 3: I shall take cooking lessons.

Rest of CHORUS of LUMBERJACKS: Don't chatter so. Let's go and eat.

(*Exeunt.*)

No. 16 Inkslinger's Regret

INKSLINGER

(*Alone*)

All the little brooks of love
    Run down towards each other.
Somewhere every valley ends,
    And loneliness is over.
Some meet early, some meet late,
    Some, like me, have long to wait.

VOICE of PAUL BUNYAN: Johnny.

INKSLINGER: Yes, Mr Bunyan.

VOICE of PAUL BUNYAN: Has anything happened since I've been away?

INKSLINGER: Keep an eye on Hel Helson. He broods too much by himself and I don't like the look on his face. And the bunch he goes around with are a bad bunch.

VOICE of PAUL BUNYAN: Poor Hel. He was born a few
    hundred years too late. Today there is no place for him.
    Anything else?
INKSLINGER: Some of the men say they are tired of logging
    and would like to settle down. They'd like to try
    farming.
VOICE of PAUL BUNYAN: John Shears?
INKSLINGER: He's the chief one but there are many others.
VOICE of PAUL BUNYAN: I'll look into it. And what about
    yourself, Johnny?
INKSLINGER: I'm all right, Mr Bunyan.
VOICE of PAUL BUNYAN: I know what you want. It's harder
    than you think and not so pleasant. But you shall have
    it and shan't have to wait much longer. Good night,
    Johnny.
INKSLINGER: Good night, Mr Bunyan.
VOICE of PAUL BUNYAN: Still *Mr* Bunyan?
INKSLINGER: Good night, Paul.

(*Exit* INKSLINGER.)

CHORUS of LUMBERJACKS: (*Offstage*) Good night, Mr
    Bunyan.
VOICE of PAUL BUNYAN: Good night. Happy dreams.

No. 17 Bunyan's Goodnight (iii)

VOICE of PAUL BUNYAN:
Now let the complex spirit dissolve in the darkness
Where the Actual and the Possible are mysteriously
    exchanged.
For the saint must descend into Hell; that his order may be
    tested by its disorder,
The hero return to the humble womb; that his will may be
    pacified and refreshed.

47

Dear children, trust the night and have faith in tomorrow,
That these hours of ambiguity and indecision may be also
the hours of healing.

ACT TWO

Scene 1
A clearing in the forest.

No. 18 Bunyan's Good Morning

VOICE of PAUL BUNYAN:
The songs of dawn have been sung and the night watchmen
 are already in the deep beginnings of sleep.

Leaning upon their implements the hired men pause to
 consider their life by the light of mid-morning, and of
 habits already established in their loosened limbs.
And the aggressive will is no longer pure.

Much has been done to prepare a continent for the
 rejoicings and recriminations of all its possible heirs.
Much has been ill done. There is never enough time to do
 more than one thing at a time, and there is always
 either too much of one thing or too little.

Virtuosos of the axe, dynamiters and huntsmen, there has
 been an excess of military qualities, of the
 resourcefulness of thieves, the camaraderie of the
 irresponsible, and the accidental beauties of silly songs.

Nevertheless you have done much to render yourselves
 unnecessary.
Loneliness has worn lines of communication.
Irrational destruction has made possible the establishment
 of a civilized order.
Drunkenness and lechery have prepared the way for a
 routine of temperance and marriage.

Already you have provoked a general impulse towards
settlement and cultivation.

(*Enter* CHORUS of LUMBERJACKS.)

CHORUS of LUMBERJACKS
What does he want to see us for?
I wonder what he has in store.
I never did a thing I shouldn't,
I couldn't. I wouldn't.
I'll do my work. I'll never shirk.
I'll never never grumble any more.

VOICE of PAUL BUNYAN: I've been thinking for some time
that we needed some farmers to grow food for the
camp, and looking around for a nice piece of country,
the other day I found the very place. A land where the
wheat grows as tall as churches and the potatoes are as
big as airships. Now those who would like to be
farmers: Stand out.

No. 18a Shears's Song

JOHN SHEARS
It has always been my dream
Since I was only so high
To live upon a farm and watch
The wheat and barley grow high.

CHORUS of FARMERS
The wheat and barley grow high.

VOICE of PAUL BUNYAN: Hel Helson.
HEL HELSON: Yes.
VOICE of PAUL BUNYAN: You are in charge while I take our
friends to the land of Heart's Desire. I want you to start

today clearing the Topsy Turvey Mountain. Now boys, if you're ready we'll start as we have a thousand miles to go before noon. But if you think farming is a soft job you'd better stay right here.

No. 18b Bunyan's Warning

VOICE of PAUL BUNYAN:
If there isn't a flood, there's a drought.
If there isn't a frost, there's a heatwave.
If it isn't the insects, it's the banks.
You'll howl more than you'll sing,
You'll frown more than you'll smile,
You'll cry more than you'll laugh.
But some people seem to like it.
Let's get going.

No. 19 Farmers' Song

JOHN SHEARS
The shanty-boy invades the wood
    Upon his cruel mission
To slay the tallest trees he can
    The height of his ambition.

FARMER 2
The farmer heeds wild Nature's cry
    For Higher Education,
And is a trusted friend to all
    The best in vegetation.

CHORUS of FARMERS
I hate to be a shanty-boy,
    I want to be a farmer,
For I prefer life's comedy
    To life's crude melodrama.

JOHN SHEARS

The shanty-boy sleeps in a bunk
    With none to call him Dad, sir,
And so you cannot wonder much
    If he goes to the bad, sir.

FARMER 2

The farmer sees his little ones
    Grow up like the green willow.
At night he has his Better Half
    Beside him on the pillow.

CHORUS of FARMERS

I hate to be a shanty-boy,
    I want to be a farmer,
For I prefer life's comedy
    To life's crude melodrama.

No. 19a Farmers' Exit

The others watch them go and all except HEL HELSON *and his* FOUR CRONIES *exeunt.*

CRONY 1: The Topsy-Turvey Mountain. It's impossible.

CRONY 2: He's nuts.

CRONY 3: Just another of his crazy ideas.

CRONY 4: You are not going to take him seriously, are you, Hel?

CRONY 1: Why do you go on taking orders from a dope like that?

CRONY 2: Why don't you run this joint yourself? We'd support you.

CRONY 3: Sure we would.

CRONY 4: Hel for Boss.

CRONY 1: Tell him where he gets off.

CRONY 2: And that stooge of his, Johnny Inkslinger.

CRONY 3: You said it. We'll take him for a ride.

CRONY 4: Stand up for your rights, Hel. You're the only boss around here.

HEL HELSON: Get out.

CRONY 1: Of course, Hel.

CRONY 2: Anything you say, boss.

CRONY 3: We were just going anyway.

CRONY 4: Don't forget what we think of you.

(*Exeunt* FOUR CRONIES. HELSON *is left sitting moodily alone.*)

No. 20 *The Mocking of Hel Helson*

HEL HELSON
Heron, heron winging by
Through the silence of the sky,
What have you heard of me, Helson the Brave?

HERON
Oh, I heard of a hero working for wages,
Taking orders just like a slave.

CHORUS
No! I'm afraid it's too late,
Helson never will be great.

HEL HELSON
Moon, moon shining bright
In the deserts of the night,
What have you heard of Helson the Fair?

MOON
Not what one should hear of one so handsome,
The girls make fun of his bashful air.

CHORUS
No! I'm afraid it's too late,
Helson never will be great.

HEL HELSON

Wind, wind as you run
Round and round the earth for fun,
What have you heard of Helson the Good?

WIND

Oh, the old story of virtue neglected,
Mocked at by others, misunderstood.

CHORUS

No! I'm afraid it's too late,
Helson never will be great.

HEL HELSON

Beetle! Beetle! Squirrel! Squirrel!
Beetle, as you pass
Down the avenues of grass,
Squirrel, as you go
Through the forests to and fro,
What have you heard of Helson the Wise? of
    Helson the Strong?

BEETLE

It's sad to think of all that wisdom
Being exploited by smarter guys.
SQUIRREL
Not what one likes to hear of a fighter,
They say he's a coward, I hope they're wrong.

CHORUS

Too late! Too late! Too late!
He will never, never, never be great!

(*Enter* FIDO, MOPPET *and* POPPET.)

MOPPET: Did you really?

POPPET: Yes, I says, excuse me, I says, but this is my roof, what of it, he says, you're trespassing, I says, and if I am, he says, who's going to stop me, yours truly, I says, scram alley cat, he says, before I eat you, I don't know about alley cats, I says, but one doesn't need to be a detective to see who has a rat in his family tree, and the fight was on.

FIDO: There now, just look. Helson has got the blues again. Dear O dear, that man has the worst inferiority complexes I've ever run across. His dreams must be amazing. Really I must ask him about them. Excuse me.

MOPPET: Nosy prig.

POPPET: He can't help it. Dogs are like that. Always sniffing.

No. 21 Fido's Sympathy

FIDO

(*Looking up at* HELSON)
Won't you tell me what's the matter?
I adore the confidential role,
Why not tell your little troubles
To a really sympathetic soul?

(HELSON *lunges a kick at him and he bolts.*)

POPPET: Dogs have no *savoir-faire*.

MOPPET: Serve him right. I hate gush.

No. 22 Cats' Creed

MOPPET and POPPET
Let Man the romantic in vision espy
A far better world than his own in the sky

55

As a tyrant or beauty express a vain wish
To be mild as a beaver or chaste as a fish.

Let the dog who's the most sentimental of all
Throw a languishing glance at the hat in the hall,
Struggle wildly to speak all the tongues that he
    hears
And to rise to the realm of Platonic ideas.

But the cat is an Aristotelian and proud
Preferring hard fact to intangible cloud;
Like the Troll in Peer Gynt, both in hunting and
    love,
The cat has one creed: 'To thyself be enough!'

POPPET: Let's go and kill birds.

MOPPET: You've heard about Tiny and Slim? Fido caught
    them necking in the pantry after breakfast.

POPPET: Yes, he told me. No one can say I'm narrow-
    minded, but there are *some* things that just aren't done
    till after dark.

(*Exeunt.*)

VOICE of PAUL BUNYAN: Helson, Helson.

(*Enter* FOUR CRONIES.)

CRONY 1: He's back.

CRONY 2: He's mad at you.

VOICE of PAUL BUNYAN: Helson, I want to talk to you.

CRONY 3: Don't pay any attention to him.

CRONY 4: Go and settle with him.

VOICE of PAUL BUNYAN: Helson.

CRONY 1: You're not going to do what he tells you, are you?

CRONY 2: Go on, wipe the floor with him.

CRONY 3: Don't let him think you're sissy.

CRONY 4: Show him you're an American. Give him the works.
HEL HELSON: I'll kill him.

(*Exit* HELSON.)

FOUR CRONIES: Atta boy.

No. 23 The Fight

(CHORUS *rush in*.)

> CHORUS
> What's happening?
> What is it?
> A fight!
> It's Helson!
> He's crazy!
> He'll kill him!
> They're heaving rocks!
> That's got him!
> No, missed him!
> Gosh! did you see that?
> Helson is tough!
> But Paul has the brains.

(*They stream out to watch the fight. Enter* SLIM *and* TINY.)

Love Duet

TINY: Slim.
SLIM: Yes, dear.
TINY: Where has everybody gone?

57

SLIM: I don't know, but I'm glad.
TINY: Darling.

(*They embrace. Thunder and shouts off.*)

SLIM

Move, move from the trysting stone,
White sun of summer depart.

TINY

That I may be left alone
With my true love close to my heart.

(*Thunder and shouts off.*)

SLIM: Tiny.
TINY: Yes, dear.
SLIM: Did you hear a funny noise?
TINY: I did, but I don't care.
SLIM: Darling.

(*They embrace.*)

TINY

The head that I love the best

SLIM

Shall lie all night on my breast

CHORUS

(*Offstage*)

Paul! Helson!
Helson is tough!
But Paul has the brains!

TINY: Slim.
SLIM: Yes, dear.
TINY: How do people really know they really are in love?

TINY and SLIM: Darling.

TINY and SLIM

Lost, lost is the world I knew,
And I have lost myself too;
Dear heart, I am lost in you.

CHORUS

(*Offstage*)

He's got him! Now!

(*Enter* CHORUS *carrying the unconscious body of* HEL HELSON.)

Mock Funeral March

CHORUS

Take away the body and lay it on the ice,
Put a lily in his hand and beef-steaks on his eyes;
Twenty tall white candles at his feet and head;
And let this epitaph be read:

Here lies an unlucky picayune;
He thought he was champ but he thought too
    soon.
Here lies Hel Helson from Scandinavia,
Rather regretting his rash behaviour.

CRONY 1

We told him not to,
We never forgot to.

CRONY 2

Be careful to say
He should obey.

CRONY 3

'Helson,' we said,
'Get this in your head,

CRONY 4

'Take orders from Paul
Or you'll have a fall.'

CRONIES 1 AND 2

We are all put here on earth for a purpose. We all have a job
to do and it is our duty to do it with all our might.

CRONIES 3 AND 4

We must obey our superiors and live according to our
station in life; for whatever the circumstances, the
Chief, the Company and the Customer are always
right.

HEL HELSON

Where am I? What happened? Am I dead?
Something struck me on the head.

CHORUS

It's all right, Hel, you're not dead,
You are lying in your bed.

HEL HELSON

Why am I so stiff and sore?
I remember nothing more.

CHORUS

All right, Hel, don't be a sap,
You'd a kind of little scrap;
Don't worry now but take a nap.

HEL HELSON

Who was it hit me on the chin?

VOICE of PAUL BUNYAN

I'm sorry, Hel, I had to do it.
I'm your friend, if you but knew it.

HEL HELSON

Good Heavens! What a fool I've been!

VOICE of PAUL BUNYAN

Let bygones be bygones. Forget the past.
We can now be friends at last.
Each of us has found a brother.
You and I both need each other.

FOUR CRONIES

That's what we always told you, Hel.

HEL HELSON

How could I ever have been so blind
As not to recognize your kind.
Now I know you. Scram. Or else.

CHORUS

Scram. Or else.

FOUR CRONIES

Ingratitude!
A purely selfish attitude!
An inability to see a joke
And characteristic of uneducated folk.

CHORUS

Scram. Or else.

FOUR CRONIES

Don't argue with them. They're sick people.

CHORUS

Scram, or else!

(*Exeunt* CRONIES.)

Hymn

VOICE of PAUL BUNYAN
Often thoughts of hate conceal
Love we are ashamed to feel;
In the climax of a fight
Lost affection comes to light.

CHORUS with HELSON
And the prisoners are set free
O great day of discovery!

TINY and SLIM
Move, move from the trysting stone,
White sun of summer depart.
That I may be left alone
With my true love close to my heart.

TINY, SLIM and CHORUS
The head that I love the best
Shall lie all night on my breast.
Lost, lost is the world I knew,
And I am lost, dear heart, in you!

HEL HELSON
Great day of discovery!

CHORUS
Great day!

62

No. 24 *Third Ballad Interlude*

NARRATOR

So Helson smiled and Bunyan smiled
And both shook hands and were reconciled.

And Paul and Johnny and Hel became
The greatest partners in the logging game.

And every day Slim and Tiny swore
They were more in love than the day before.

All over the States the stories spread
Of Bunyan's camp and the life they led.

Of fights with Indians, of shooting matches,
Of monster bears and salmon catches.

Of the whirling whimpus Paul fought and killed,
Of the Buttermilk Line that he had to build.

And a hundred other tales were known
From Nantucket Island to Oregon.

From the Yiddish Alps to the Rio Grande,
From the Dust Bowl down to the Cotton Land.

In every dialect and tongue
His tales were told and his stories sung,

Harsh in the Bronx where they cheer with zest,
With a burring R in the Middle West,

And lilting and slow in Arkansas
Where instead of Father they say Paw.

63

But there came a winter, these stories say,
When Babe came up to Paul one day,

Stood still and looked him in the eye;
Paul said nothing for he knew why.

'Shoulder your axe and leave this place:
Let the clerk move in with his well-washed face.

'Let the architect with his sober plan
Build a residence for the average man;

'And garden birds not bat an eye
When locomotives whistle by;

'And telephone wires go from town to town
For lovers to whisper sweet nothings down.*

'We must depart – but it's Christmas Eve –
So let's have a feast before we leave.'

That is all I have to tell,
The party's starting; friends, farewell.

Scene 2

No. 25 The Christmas Party

*Christmas Eve. A full-size pine-tree lit up as a Christmas
tree in background. Foreground a big table with candles.*
CHORUS *eating dinner. Funny hats, streamers, noises.*

*Optional cut.

Another slice of turkey, another slice of ham,
I'll feel sick to-morrow, but I don't give a damn.
Take a quart of whiskey and mix it with your beer,
Pass the gravy, will you? Christmas comes but once
　　a year.

FIDO

Men are three parts crazy and no doubt always
　　were,
But why do they go mad completely one day in the
　　year?

CHORUS

Who wants the Pope's nose? I do.
French fried if you please,
I've a weakness for plum pudding.
Would you pass the cheese?
Wash it down with Bourbon.
I think I'll stick to Rye.
There's nothing to compare with real old-fashioned
　　pie.

MOPPET and POPPET

Seeing his temper's so uncertain, it's very queer,
He should always be good-tempered one day in the
　　year.

CHORUS

Cigars!
Hurrah!
Some nuts!
I'm stuffed to here!
Your health!
Skol!
Prosit!

Santé!
Cheers!
A merry, merry Christmas and a happy New Year.

(INKSLINGER *bangs on the table and rises*.)

INKSLINGER

Dear friends, with your leave this Christmas Eve
    I rise to make a pronouncement;
Some will have guessed but I thought it best
    To make an official announcement.

Hot Biscuit Slim, you all know him,
    As your cook (or *coquus* in Latin)
Has been put in charge of a very large
    Hotel in Mid-Manhattan.

(*Cheers*.)

But Miss Tiny here, whom we love so dear,
    I understand has now consented
To share his life as his loving wife.
    They both look very contented.

THREE SOLOS from CHORUS

Carry her over the water,
    Set her down under the tree,
Where the culvers white all day and all night,
    And the winds from every quarter,
Sing agreeably, agreeably, agreeably of love.

FIDO, MOPPET and POPPET

Put a gold ring on her finger,
    Press her close to your heart,
While the fish in the lake their snapshots take,

66

And the frog, that sanguine singer,
Sings agreeably, agreeably, agreeably of love.

The preacher shall dance at your marriage,
    The steeple bend down to look,
The pulpit and chairs shed suitable tears,
    While the horses drawing your carriage
Sing agreeably, agreeably, agreeably of love.

TINY and SLIM

(*Rising*)

Where we are is not very far
    To walk from Grand Central Station,
If you ever come East, you will know at least
    Of a standing invitation.

(*They sit down.*)

INKSLINGER
And Hel so tall who managed for Paul
    And had the task of converting
His ambitious dreams into practical schemes
    And of seeing we all were working,

Will soon be gone to Washington
    To join the Administration
As a leading man in the Federal Plan
    Of public works for the nation.

(*Cheers.* HELSON *rises.*)

HEL HELSON
I hope that some of you will come
    To offer your assistance

In installing turbines and High Tension lines
And bringing streams from a distance.

(*Cheers. He sits down.*)

INKSLINGER
And now three cheers for old John Shears
Who has taken a short vacation
From his cattle and hay, to be with us today
On this important occasion.

(*Cheers.* JOHN SHEARS *rises.*)

JOHN SHEARS
(*Stammering*)
I am . . . I'm not . . . er which, er what . . .
As I was saying . . . the er . . .
The er . . . the well, I mean, O Hell,
I'm mighty glad to be here.

(*Cheers. He sits down.*)

WESTERN UNION BOY
(*Offstage*)
Inkslinger! John Inkslinger!

(*Enter* WESTERN UNION BOY *on his bicycle.*)

A telegram, a telegram,
A telegram from Hollywood.
Inkslinger is the name;
And I think that the news is good.

INKSLINGER: (*Reading*) 'Technical Adviser required for
all-star lumber picture stop your name suggested stop if
interested wire collect stop.'

INKSLINGER

A lucky break, am I awake?
    Please pinch me if I'm sleeping.
It only shows that no one knows
    The future of bookkeeping.

CHORUS

We always knew that one day you
    Would come to be famous, Johnny.
When you're prosperous remember us
    And we'll all sing Hey Nonny, Nonny.

INKSLINGER

And last of all I call on Paul
    To speak to us this evening,
I needn't say how sad today
    We are that he is leaving.

Every eye is ready to cry
    At the thought of bidding adieu, sir,
For sad is the heart when friends must part,
    But enough – I call upon you, sir.

No. 26 *Bunyan's Farewell*

VOICE of PAUL BUNYAN:
Now the task that made us friends
In a common labour, ends;
For an emptiness is named
And a wilderness is tamed
Till its savage nature can
Tolerate the life of man.

All I had to do is done,
You remain but I go on;
Other kinds of deserts call,

Other forests whisper Paul;
I must hasten to reply
To that low instinctive cry,
There to make a way again
For the conscious lives of men.

Here, though, is your life, and here
The pattern is already clear
That machinery imposes
On you as the frontier closes,
Gone the natural disciplines
And the life of choice begins.

You and I must go our way;
I have but one word to say:
O remember, friends, that you
Have the harder task to do
As at freedom's puzzled feet
Yawn the gulfs of self-defeat;
All but heroes are unnerved
When life and love must be deserved.

No. 27 *Litany*

CHORUS
The campfire embers are black and cold,
The banjos are broken, the stories are told,
The woods are cut down, and the young grown
  old.

FIDO, MOPPET and POPPET
From a Pressure Group that says I am the
  Constitution,
From those who say Patriotism and mean
  Persecution,

From a Tolerance that is really inertia and
    disillusion:

CHORUS
Save animals and men.

TINY and SLIM: Bless us, father.
VOICE of PAUL BUNYAN:
A father cannot bless.
May you find the happiness that you possess.

CHORUS
The echoing axe shall be heard no more
Nor the rising scream of the buzzer saw
Nor the crash as the ice-jam explodes in the thaw.

FIDO, MOPPET and POPPET
From entertainments neither true nor beautiful nor
    witty,
From a homespun humour manufactured in the
    city,
From the dirty-mindedness of a Watch Committee:

CHORUS
Save animals and men.

HEL HELSON: Don't leave us, Paul. What's to become of
    America now?
VOICE of PAUL BUNYAN:
Every day America's destroyed and re-created,
America is what you do,
America is I and you,
America is what you choose to make it.

71

CHORUS

No longer the logger shall hear in the Fall
The pine and the spruce and the sycamore call.

VOICE of PAUL BUNYAN: Goodbye, dear friends.

CHORUS

Goodbye, Paul.

FIDO, MOPPET and POPPET

From children brought up to believe in self-
expression,
From the theology of plumbers or the medical
profession,
From depending on alcohol for self-respect and
self-possession:

CHORUS

Save animals and men.

INKSLINGER: Paul, who are you?
VOICE of PAUL BUNYAN:
Where the night becomes the day,
Where the dream becomes the fact,
I am the Eternal Guest,
I am Way,
I am Act.

Appendix A

CHORUS 1: Ah that music. How lovely it is. Louder. More. More.
CHORUS 2: Let me dream I am the master of a goddess.
CHORUS 3: Let me dream I am the little owner of a luxurious garden.
CHORUS 4: Let me land on a calm shore where I have been long expected.
CHORUS 5: Let me be a drowned hero without a wish.

(*Enter* DREAM SHADOWS, FILM STARS *and* MODELS.)

No. 17 Lullaby

CHORUS

Say O say farewell
Now is yesterday
But the tolling of a bell
On a fading, fading shore:

Gaze and fear no more
Into sleep's translucent wave
Deeper, deeper, deeper still;
All the motions of your will
Given to its oceans, hear
Like the drumming of an ear
Sorrows homing to their grave.

(*Sound of snores.*)

DREAM SHADOW 1: All OK.
DREAM SHADOW 2: Ssh. Not so loud.
VOICE: (*Offstage*) Go on singing, ma.

DREAM SHADOW 3: O damn. Excuse me. (*Runs off stage.*) Go to sleep this minute or I'll give you such a nightmare. (*Returns.*) Phew.

DREAM SHADOW 3: A moment's peace at last.

DREAM SHADOW 2: O these men.

DREAM SHADOW 1: They seem to think we enjoy entertaining them.

DREAM SHADOW 4: Gosh, I could do with a vacation.

DREAM SHADOWS
You've no idea how dull it is
Just being perfect nullities,
     The idols of a democratic nation;
The heroes of the multitude
Their dreams of female pulchritude:
     We're very very tired of admiration.

DREAM SHADOW 3
The cut of my moustache and lips,

DREAM SHADOW 1
My measurement around the hips,

DREAM SHADOWS 1 and 3
Obey the whims of fashion;

DREAM SHADOW 3
In our embraces we select
Whatever technique seems correct

DREAM SHADOW 1
To give the visual effect

DREAM SHADOWS 1 and 3
Of an Eternal Passion.

DREAM SHADOW 2
On beaches or in night-clubs I
Excel at femininity,

DREAM SHADOW 4
And I at all athletics;

DREAM SHADOW 2
I pay attention to my hair,

DREAM SHADOW 4
For personal hygiene I've a flair,

DREAM SHADOW 2
The Hercules of underwear,

DREAM SHADOW 4
The Venus of cosmetics.

DREAM SHADOWS
We're bored with being glamorous,
We're bored with being amorous,
    For all our fans we don't give a banana;
Who wants to be exhibited
To all the world's inhibited
    As representative Americana.

DREAM SHADOW 2
The things a man of eighty-two
Will ask of his dream *ingénue*
    I shouldn't like to retail;

DREAM SHADOW 1
Unless you tried to play mama.
You can't think how particular

Young men who miss their mothers are
   About each little detail.

DREAM SHADOW 4
Rescuing girls from waterfalls
Or shooting up the sheriff, palls,
   Like any violent action;

DREAM SHADOW 3
We never want to fly again
Or throw a custard pie again
To give the decent citizen
   Vicarious satisfaction.

DREAM SHADOWS
The growth of social consciousness
Has failed to make our problems less,
   Indeed, they grow intenser;
And what with Freud and what with Marx
With bureaucrats and matriarchs
The chances are our little larks
   Will not get past the censor.

You'd hate it if you were employed
To be a sin in celluloid
   Or else a saint in plaster;
O little hearts who make a fuss,
What pleasure it would give to us
To give the bird to Oedipus,
   The raspberry to Jocasta.

You've no idea how dull it is
Just being perfect nullities,
   The idols of a democratic nation;
The heroes of the multitude,

Their dreams of female pulchritude;
We're VERY VERY tired of admiration.

CHORUS

(*Offstage*)
Gaze and fear no more
Into sleep's translucent wave
Deeper, deeper, deeper still;
All the motions of your will
Given to its oceans, hear
Like the drumming of an ear
Sorrows homing to their grave.

(*Sound of heavy snores.*)

Appendix B

CHORUS
But how do you think we should address her
What can we do to impress her?
INKSLINGER
You must sing her a love song.
CHORUS
That's too hard and takes too long.
INKSLINGER: Nonsense. It's quite easy, and the longer it is,
the more she'll like it. Use the longest words you can
think of. Like this:

No. 15 *The Love Song*

INKSLINGER

In this emergency
Of so much urgency,
    What can I do
Except wax lyrical?
Don't look satirical;
I have empirical
    Proof I love you.

Like statisticians, I
Distrust magicians, I
    Think them a crew,
That is, collectively;
Speaking objectively
If not effectively,
I feel protectively
    Mad about you.

Speaking with deference,
I have a preference

For a nice view:
Your look of spaciousness,
Your manner's graciousness,
Your limb's vivaciousness,
Your mind's herbaceousness
Your whole palatiousness
    Makes me love you.

Some force mysteriously
But most imperiously
    Warms my heart through:
I on detecting it,
After inspecting it
Find that correcting it
Will mean reflecting it,
Back and convecting it,
In fact connecting it
    Firmly with you.

You must receive it: a
natural *naïveté*
    Tells me to woo:
Please don't sarcastically
Iconoclastically
Say I'm bombastically
Telling a drastic lie;
Hardly monastically,
Quite orgiastically
I dream fantastically
    Often of you.

My dreams compulsively,
Almost convulsively
    Show it is true:
No animosity,
Only precocity:

Eyes' luminosity
Ears' curiosity
Nose's monstrosity
Cheeks' adiposity
And lips' verbosity
All with velocity
    Bear down on you.

INKSLINGER: Got the idea? Right. Now this time you join
    in. When I think of a word, you think of another word
    to rhyme with it.

INKSLINGER

All nouns are dedicate
To this one predicate
    Adjective too:
Appendicectomy

CHORUS

's a pain in the neck to me

INKSLINGER

Anthropomorphosis

CHORUS

Owns several offices

INKSLINGER

Psychokinesia

CHORUS

Never gets easier

INKSLINGER

Papal Encyclicals

80

Are full of pricklicles

Plenipotentiaries

CHORUS
Endure for centuries

INKSLINGER
Supralapsarians

CHORUS
Aren't vegetarians

INKSLINGER
Hendecasyllable

CHORUS
Makes me feel illable

INKSLINGER
Icthyosauruses

CHORUS
Won't sing in choruses

INKSLINGER
Septuagesima

CHORUS
Ate less and lessima

INKSLINGER
Occi-parietal

O DO BE QUIET

all

Mean:

I LOVE YOU.

THE ORIGINS, EVOLUTION AND
METAMORPHOSES OF *PAUL BUNYAN*,
AUDEN'S AND BRITTEN'S
'AMERICAN' OPERA

by
Donald Mitchell

To Philip Brunelle and Simon Foster

Prefatory Note

The text of *Paul Bunyan* which is published here represents in all essentials the libretto of Britten's operetta, first performed in New York in 1941 and revised by the composer in 1974 for its first European performances in 1976. I include, however, as two appendices, the texts of two numbers which were heard in 1941 but omitted in 1974. This means that we have access to a text of the libretto as performed in 1941 which at the same time respects the composer's final thoughts about his youthful operetta.

My introduction naturally focuses on the text as we know it in relation to Britten's music. It does not pretend to be a critical edition of the libretto alone. This is the task of Professor Edward Mendelson, who at the time of writing has in preparation a volume of Auden's libretti and other dramatic works (1939–73), the second volume in the complete edition of the poet's works that he is editing.

D.M.

London, 1987

In May 1939, Benjamin Britten, accompanied by Peter Pears, left England for North America. They had been preceded by their friends, W. H. Auden and Christopher Isherwood, who had crossed the Atlantic in January. Auden and Isherwood were to stay in the States and become American citizens. Britten and Pears, after their three years' temporary residence, were to return home, to wartime England, in March 1942.

Auden and Britten had been close collaborators in England in the thirties, above all in their work at the GPO Film Unit, the organization that first brought them together in 1935. But it was not only in documentary films like *Coal Face* and *Night Mail* that their extraordinary talents were combined. They also worked together in the theatre, in Rupert Doone's Group Theatre, where Britten wrote much incidental (and integral) music for Auden's and Isherwood's plays, *The Ascent of F6* and *On the Frontier*, and again in the then relatively new medium of radio: it was for the BBC that Auden and Britten wrote (in 1937) a pioneering and still remembered radio feature, *Hadrian's Wall*. And, finally, there were the works for the concert hall, for example *On this Island* (1937), Britten's settings of poems from Auden's *Look, Stranger!* (1936), and, yet more elaborate and audacious, the orchestral song-cycle *Our Hunting Fathers* (1936).

In retrospect, their joint activity in the thirties in film, theatre and radio appears exhilarating, fresh and adventurous. Some of its manifestations wore a political or quasi-political face. But we should not allow wrangles about the prudence or sincerity of thirties political convictions to mask a significant and enduring aspect of the collaboration, that it was specifically in these thirties 'media' areas that Britten began to learn his trade as a musical dramatist. These were areas, moreover, in which calls were often made on his knack for writing music in a popular vein (sometimes as a vehicle for satire). It was experience – an extension of his vocabulary – that he was to find useful in America.

After *Paul Bunyan*, Britten was not to work again with

Auden in the musical theatre. But Auden himself, with his abiding commitment to music, was to go on to write librettos (with Chester Kallman) for Stravinsky, Henze and Nicolas Nabokov (and to make a translation of the libretto of Mozart's *Magic Flute*). Thus his first essay in this field is of unique interest and importance.

We also have to remind ourselves that *Paul Bunyan* was Britten's first full-length work for the theatre, so overshadowed was it by the phenomenal success of *Peter Grimes* four years later. Overshadowed, of course, because unknown.

The first performance of *Bunyan*, which was given by the Columbia Theater Associates of Columbia University, New York (with the co-operation of the university's department of music), took place at Brander Matthews Hall on 5 May 1941, after which it was clear to the composer and poet that some revisions were obligatory. These they began to attend to; but by the end of the year Britten and Pears had decided to return to England, finally making the voyage home by boat in March 1942. Meanwhile, in the summer of 1941, which they spent in California, they had alighted on Crabbe's poem *The Borough*, and the idea of a new opera, *Peter Grimes*, was born.

That was certainly one reason why further thought about *Bunyan* was abandoned. There was also the physical separation from Auden, from the North American context, from the culture with which, through *Bunyan*, Britten had attempted to identify himself. There were other works from his American years in which it is evident that he was deliberately seeking to establish and exploit an authentically American 'voice'. Britten would have thought it strange *not* to address American audiences in a language, a musical language, that would have offered them immediately comprehensible cultural references. *Paul Bunyan*, at least from the composer's point of view, represents the most thoroughgoing of these American immersions, the conscious employment of an idiom based on the popular American music of the day. Hence, undoubtedly, the proliferation of Broadway chorus numbers, solo songs and duets in a popular style, the role allotted the blues, and so on; and Auden was no less dextrous in finding ingenious, funny, witty and moving words and rhymes to match dramatic or lyrical incidents that often had more to do with the 'musical' than music drama. Britten himself, when writing home from the States to his sister Beth on 19 October 1939, makes a point of the Broadway connection:

> I see lots of Wystan: it is nice to have him around . . . Wystan and my opera is settled for Broadway *when* we have done it. We'll have our work cut out doing it, I feel!

And on the very same day he was writing to his publisher in London, Ralph Hawkes, of Boosey & Hawkes,

> Auden and I are set now to write a school operetta for Max Winkler [at the time the head of the Boosey & Hawkes office in New York]. This has the extra stimulus of a possible professional Broadway performance by the well-known Ballet Caravan in January. This seems an excellent thing, since it is a first-rate start for a work of this kind, and also before the work is printed we can have practical experience of how the work sounds and looks on the stage. The probable subject is that of Paul Bunyan, the American frontier hero, who has, believe me, the most extraordinary adventures. It is certainly up Wystan's tree and also up mine.

Work continued in November and December. On 11 November Peter Pears wrote to a friend, 'Ben is working hard, an opera for Broadway in January . . .', and on the 21st there was news from Britten to Hawkes that the first act was completed:

> He [Wystan] is coming down tomorrow with it to discuss it and I will find out how he has cast Paul Bunyan's feet.

However, I gather that Paul Bunyan never appears on the stage, so that avoids the problem of his size of boot. It is excellent that Auden is associated with us over it, since he has a very big name over here.

This was probably the first indication of what turned out to be a feature of the concept of the opera which was widely criticized at the time – the non-appearance of the mythical hero, the giant logger, in any other form except as a speaking voice. (It is my view that with the resources of modern technology available to us, Auden's bold gamble can now at last be brought off in a way that he could only have dreamt of.)

On 8 December Britten was writing to Wulff, the son of Hermann Scherchen, 'I see Wystan an awful lot . . . You know I'm writing an operetta with him to be put on at the end of January? It's very good so far (at least *his* part is – customary modesty (!))', and at the end of the month, to his sister Beth, 'Wystan has been here for a week – we've done lots of work on the opera – I know you'd like it – it's full of nice tunes and blues and things. No date for a production yet.' On 5 January, from Chicago, where he was appearing as soloist in the American première of his Piano Concerto, Britten wrote back to Elizabeth Mayer at Amityville, '. . . I did take time off this morning to try to get some work done on P.B. Goodness what a breath of fresh air that stuff of Wystan's seems . . .' (It was in 1963 that Auden wrote, 'I have, alas, no talent for writing memoirs, for if I had, I would devote a whole chapter to a house in Amityville, Long Island, the home of Dr William and Elizabeth Mayer, where Benjamin Britten and Peter Pears stayed in 1939–40; a house which played an important role in the lives of all three of us. It was during this period that Britten wrote his first opera, and I my first libretto, on the subject of an American folk hero, Paul Bunyan.' See also p. 148.)

By 16 January the first full typescript of the libretto was ready, but Britten was writing to Beth at the end of the month, 'No date for production yet!', an exclamation that proved to be prophetic in more ways than one. Not only did the performance not take place as planned in January 1940 – the opera in fact was not completed until 1941 – but the first performance, on 5 May of that year, was not given on Broadway but on a university campus. No doubt the collapse of the hopes for a Broadway production contributed to the postponement of the opera's completion, but it was also the case that in 1940 Britten had a bout of severe illness early in the year and was heavily preoccupied with commissions with a deadline date attached to them, most notably the *Sinfonia da Requiem*, written for the 2600th anniversary of the Japanese Empire and ultimately rejected by the commissioning committee: it was Auden who helped Britten draft a letter expressing the composer's surprise at the upshot of this tragi-comic affair.

But though a Broadway first night may not have materialized, and whether or not one concludes that it was a sensible or realistic ambition in the first place, there can be no denying that the Broadway idea (or goal) had a vital influence on the shaping of *Paul Bunyan* and was responsible for some of its most prominent features. The catchy chorus numbers, for example, with which Britten so prodigally littered his score, some of which are brilliant exercises in (*not* parodies of) the Broadway manner, e.g. the Lumberjacks' Chorus (No. 4), or the Food Chorus (No. 11), a topic of the first importance to Auden which excited him to ever more extravagant and unpredictable imagery:

> Do I look the sort of fellow
> Whom you might expect to bellow
>   For a quail in aspic, or
> Who would look at glum as Gandhi
> If he wasn't offered brandy
>   With a Lobster Thermidor?
>
> Who would howl like some lost sinner
> For a sherry before dinner,

And demand a savoury;
Who would criticize the stuffing
In the olives, and drink nothing
But Lapsang Suchong tea?

The importance of food, as it happens, is established along with Johnny Inkslinger's first appearance. Johnny, the camp's bookkeeper and scribe, represents thinking, literate man and the life of the mind – imagination and creativity. But Paul briskly has to remind him of life's economic realities:

VOICE of PAUL BUNYAN: How are you going to pay for
     your supper?
INKSLINGER: Dunno. Never thought of it.
VOICE of PAUL BUNYAN:
If you work for me
You shall eat splendidly
But no work, no pay.

But food is by no means just a subject for comic treatment, though it also gives rise to the funny Cooks' Duet (No. 7) – 'Sam for soups, Ben for beans' – which manages not only to satirize the absurdities of nineteenth-century 'operatic' conventions (in the manner of Donizetti) but interpolates some wonderfully sharp and mocking parodies of an advertising culture that plays on fears of commercial and physical inadequacy:

The Best People are crazy about soups!

Beans are all the rage among the Higher Income
     Groups!

Do you feel a left-out at parties,
when it comes to promotion are you passed over,
and does your wife talk in her sleep?

Then ask our nearest agent
to tell you about soups for success!

It was not only Britten who had an acute ear when it came to the art of parody, the success of which much depends on the authenticity of *accent*; and here Auden and Britten were often perfectly matched as writer and musician. (The spontaneous laughter on the private recording made of one of the 1941 performances shows how keenly relished by the audience were these particular satirical shafts.)

The Cooks' Duet and later Food Chorus (No. 11) bring us food in the context of dreadful cooking, but like all the best comedies *Paul Bunyan* shows us that laughter is rarely the whole truth. The theme of food – but this time spelled out as a basic human need (and a basic human right) – provides the refrain of what is undoubtedly the most important solo number in the work, Johnny Inkslinger's Song (No. 14):

It was out in the sticks that the fire
    Of my existence began,
Where no one had heard the *Messiah*
    And no one had seen a Cézanne.

Each strophe of his song concludes with the refrain, 'But I guess that a guy gotta eat', which is itself a vocal version of the song's basic motive, a cadencing sequence of three chords on the xylophone and celesta. Johnny's pertinent observation, in the song's sublime coda, is converted into a sentiment, the universality and compassion of which transcends his personal predicament (the 'creative' individual finding his place and useful employment in society):

Oh, but where are those beautiful places
    Where what you begin you complete,

93

> Where the joy shines out of men's faces,
> And all get sufficient to eat?*

An echo there, surely, of the social conscience of the thirties which had been so much part of Auden's and Britten's thinking in pre-war England, a conscience that had also formed an important part of the philosophy, policies and politics of the Roosevelt years, of the New Deal. It was the tail-end of that extraordinary period that provided Auden and Britten with their working environment until Pearl Harbor and the outbreak of the Pacific war finally put paid to the momentum that had created the Works Progress Administration and Federal Theater and many similar projects. The process of dismantlement and cut-back had in fact started earlier but enough remained for something of the social ideals and aspirations of the America of the New Deal to influence the character and content of *Paul Bunyan*.

As soon as one starts introducing the word 'sublime' into the discussion, then it seems that we have drifted far from the characteristics of Broadway with which we are familiar – glitz, glamour, spectacle, frivolity, to name only four. And if we look back to 1930 and a vintage Gershwin show, *Girl Crazy*, then two things strike us, first the marvellous, irresistible score and second the (now) unsalvageably inane book. But as

---

*In an earlier draft, the last four lines were quite other:

> Yet I dream of a day when employment
> Will be not such a difficult feat,
> When by doing what gives him enjoyment
> A guy gets sufficient to eat.

There is an indication on the page that these lines were to be omitted and a new text substituted – the lines in fact that Britten was to set. Interestingly, the new text is written out in the margin in the composer's hand, not Auden's; and the amendment suggests to me that the devising of a new text was in response to a musical requirement. Certainly the somewhat flat and trite sentiment of the lines as first drafted, albeit they represent what we know to be Johnny's *idée fixe*, could not have led to the song's extraordinary coda that I describe above. It is my guess that Britten needed something of a visionary, humanist nature to round off the song, and got it from his collaborator.

the era of the Great Depression and New Deal advanced, so too did Broadway open up to new influences, to new ideas. The ideal of entertainment was not abandoned, but as we can see from Gershwin's own career and the increasing scope and range of his art, from *Lady, Be Good!* (1924) to *Strike Up the Band* (1930), *Of Thee I Sing* (1931) and *Porgy and Bess* (1935), Broadway too had become involved in that general movement in the arts in America which took the nation itself – its power, glories, triumphs, ambiguities, failures and defeats – as a subject for celebration and scepticism (America has always been wonderfully strong in self-criticism). In some important respects *Paul Bunyan*, both libretto and music, was built into this tradition of quest and questioning; and it is no accident that the work's concluding Litany sobers us all up after the charm and exuberance of the Christmas Party (with the ritual summons to Hollywood delivered to Inkslinger by a Western Union messenger boy, *deus ex machina*, astride his bicycle) with its interpolated pleas for delivery

> From a Pressure Group that says I am the
>   Constitution,
> From those who say Patriotism and mean
>   Persecution,
> From a Tolerance that is really inertia and
>   disillusion
>   Save animals and men.

(If one is surprised to find animals incorporated into the texts of the chants – a form of petitioning that would have had its roots in Auden's and Britten's Anglican church-going youth – they are there because animals have had important roles to play in the operetta.)

The very final pages of the work pose the final question:

HELSON: Don't leave us Paul. What's to become of America now?

VOICE of PAUL BUNYAN:
Every day America's destroyed and re-created,
America is what you do,
America is I and you,
America is what you choose to make it.

(In the first series of performances the actor playing Paul introduced – intentionally or unintentionally – a telling modification: 'America is what *we* choose to make it'.* The point would not have been lost on an audience in New York in 1941.)

In some sense to define 'America': that was certainly an important part of what *Paul Bunyan* was seriously about; and in the strangest way, this very ambition, which understandably must have struck at least some among the work's first audiences in 1941 as insufferably opinionated and bumptious, now lends the opera its extraordinary topicality. The music critic of *Time* (19 May), reviewing the first performance, referred to an 'anaemic operetta put up by two British expatriates' that was 'as bewildering and irritating a treatment of the outsize lumberman as any two Englishmen could have devised'. But now, in the eighties, we find the questions asked and the issues raised throughout *Bunyan* still claiming our attention, still requiring resolution. If anything, the questions

---

*However, a discarded early draft for a pre-Prologue prologue (!) reads:

> And America? Well,
> Only our dreams can tell.
> They say that every day
> America's destroyed and re-created
> By what we are and what we do:
> America is I and you;
> Like dreams, America is what we make it.

At a later stage, an amended version of these lines was to form the very end of the operetta, but they were replaced by the present text for Bunyan, 'Where the night becomes the day', which had previously been located where the meditation on America is now sited.

have become yet more urgent. Johnny's seeking after those beautiful places where 'all get sufficient to eat' strikes a peculiarly resonant and powerful note amid the famines of the 1980s; and there are a dozen other topics touched on, some lightly and wittily, some gravely, in grand rhetoric, which are as much live issues today as they were in the thirties and forties: the struggle between brain and brawn; the conflict between order and disorder, discipline and indiscipline; the role of the intellectual; the nature of 'civilization', and its impact on the ecology of the world we inhabit; the recognition of a world inhabited by animals *and* men; and, not least, the generation gap, with youth (Young Trees) rebelling against age (Old Trees) and provoking the latter to a politicized panic response –

> Reds. They're sick.
> Reds. Such nonsense. It's only a phase.
> Reds. They're crazy. Nonsense. Reds.

– a phenomenon that is still with us as our battered century moves to its close. After the clearing of the great forests by the loggers, after the 'taming' of Nature – what? Paul Bunyan has an answer: 'the life of choice begins'. One might argue that the opera itself is all about choice – 'America is what you [we] choose to make it.' Not only America, as we know from our own post-war traumas. This is one of the paradoxical strengths of the opera that its authors could hardly have foreseen: its enduring timeliness.

It would not be useful to deny that in a significant sense *Paul Bunyan* as often departs from its Broadway models as it adheres to them. But the point I want to make is that Broadway itself, at least at the height of the New Deal, was making more than an occasional gesture in the direction of social context and commentary, and thus *Paul Bunyan*, from one point of view, was merely following already established precedents. Broadway and the whole world of the musical and popular song already commanded a formidable sophistication, in the music and, more especially, in the lyrics. However vacuous the story-line might be, the individual lyrics were often astonishingly elegant and witty in their formulation, urbane in their thinking and wide and demanding in their range of reference. Inkslinger's Song, indeed, which names and juxtaposes in a long sequence the *Messiah*, Cézanne, Keats, Tolstoy, Sanskrit, the history of Spain, St Sebastian, the temples of Crete, and an anonymous D major Sonata (for which Britten obligingly produces the matching tonality), stands in the brilliant textual tradition of Ira Gershwin and, say, Cole Porter (the latter much admired by Auden and Britten and imitated by them in their Cabaret Songs), and so is not as remote from traditional 'entertainment' in the thirties and forties as on first sight it might seem to be. As for the music, it is markedly simple in construction, a strophic song with the haunting refrain I have mentioned earlier unforgettably translated in the coda, but not that far removed, one might think, from the settings of Auden (*On This Island*, Op. 11) which Britten had composed in 1937 before he left for the USA. The emphatic simplicity at least we can attribute to the composer's determination not to stray too far from the norms of the convention within which he and his librettist were working.

But if Inkslinger's Song, in its complexity of feeling, stands somewhat detached from the Broadway genre (and from a purely musical point of view its innovative orchestration – no strings! – runs entirely counter to the typical Broadway sound), there are other numbers, for example, Tiny's Song (No. 15a) and Slim's Song (No. 12a), which are rooted in the American popular musical theatre. Slim's, the cowboy's, song brilliantly evokes an open-air, rolling prairie-land atmosphere in music which reminds us of nothing so much as hits from *Oklahoma!*, say, or *Annie Get Your Gun* – until one remembers that those shows date respectively from 1943 (Rodgers and Hammerstein) and 1946 (Berlin and Fields). This is not to claim that *Paul Bunyan* was a precursor of later and greater musicals. On the contrary, the chronology shows with what ingenuity Britten and Auden occupied a specifically American musical space, a territory that had already been defined and which, long after *Paul Bunyan* had been first performed and then virtually forgotten, was to be further exploited, to great popular acclaim on both sides of the Atlantic. (We should remember too that the pursuit of an open-air, native American music – something immediately recognizable as 'American' in spirit, place and character – was not confined to Broadway. It also formed part of the aesthetic of a 'serious' composer, like Aaron Copland, to whom Britten was close during the years he spent in the States.)

Both Slim's Song (especially in its exuberant accompanimental syncopations) and Tiny's (in its (string-based!) sentiment) are direct in their appeal and make a bid to catch the general ear, though it was certainly not from Broadway that the coda to Tiny's number was derived. It was hardly like this that popular songs concluded in the thirties and forties:

> The white bone
> Lies alone
> Like the limestone
> Under the green grass.
> All time goes by;
> We too shall lie
> Under death's eye.
> Alas, alas.

(This coda, incidentally, Britten brilliantly modified in 1975 and brought to its present shape, without any amendment of Auden's words.)

The stepping in and out of a straightforward popular musical idiom (in both text and music) is one of the most fascinating features of *Paul Bunyan*. Initially it may well have contributed to the general incomprehension with which the

rk was greeted in 1941, but now may prove to be one of its
:ing strengths. In any event one may be sure that these
ernations in the opera's idiomatic current accurately reflect
e personalities and ambitions of poet and composer, who
uld hardly have been content with a complacent replica of
e going Broadway idiom.

These challenging juxtapositions sometimes emerge from
e sequence of numbers (I doubt that the stylistic contrasts
ere consciously contrived) and sometimes occur within the
independent number. The magnificent choral Prologue
(No. 2), for example, unfolds a heart-stopping number for the
chorus, 'Once in a while', which any whole-hogging Broad-
way composer of the day would have been delighted to hijack.
(It is not only here, by the way, that Britten perfectly hits off
the Broadway voice. The solo interpolations too have about
them the unmistakable tone of musical comedy.) 'Once in a
while' is a marvellous inspiration, authentically born of the
'musical', and yet born too out of the limpid chorus which
opens the Prologue –

> Since the birth
> Of the earth
> Time has gone
> On and on

– the classic triadic simplicity of which (with its prophetic
juxtapositions of C major and E major!) we may feel has more
to do with another and more famous Auden setting, the *Hymn
to St Cecilia*, which would seem to occupy another world
altogether. Impossible that the worlds of the Saint and
Broadway should rub shoulders? But they do in the Prologue
to *Paul Bunyan* and are very ingeniously (motivically) inte-
grated besides. And not only those worlds, but also the
musics of East and West – it is in the Prologue, Figs. 11–12,
that we encounter Britten's first heterophonic brush with Bali,
through the mediation of a fellow composer, Colin McPhee,

Love duet.

Move, move from the trysting stone,
White sun of summer, depart
That I may be left alone
With my true love close to my heart

The heart that I love the best
Shall lie all night on my breast

Lost, Lost
Gone, gone is the world I knew
But I have lost myself too
Dear heart, I am lost in you.

The text of the Love Duet for Tiny and Slim which forms part
of The Fight, in Auden's hand

The melody of the Love Duet in Britten's hand (see also List of Illustrations, 3)

an early application, one might think, of what has now become fashionable as minimalism.

Bold juxtaposition is a feature of other numbers, for example the highly dramatic (and operatic!) choral commentary on the fight between Bunyan and Helson, in and out of which emerge Slim's and Tiny's avowals of love, the accents of which (text and music) are unmistakably those of the musical:

SLIM: Tiny.
TINY: Yes, dear.
SLIM: Did you hear a funny noise?
TINY: I did, but I don't care.
SLIM: Darling.
(*They embrace.*)

The popular-style Love Duet is reintroduced with thrilling effect in the celebratory Hymn ('O great day of discovery'), as counterpoint to a ritualistic ostinato which clearly derives from the finale of Stravinsky's *Symphony of Psalms*, a work Britten much admired. We meet here a precise example of the mix of idioms that the first audience of *Paul Bunyan* perhaps found puzzling. It is also something else: a recapitulation of the 'big tune' which was certainly not unknown to the Broadway show but which now strikes us, no doubt with the benefit of hindsight, as just the kind of ingenious climactic gesture that we would expect of a budding musical dramatist. Indeed, as *Paul Bunyan* progresses it is fascinating to observe how the work increasingly spills over into the forms and manners of the straight musical theatre, how the show, the operetta – call it what you will – more nearly approaches what we recognize as opera. Wherever the libretto offers an appropriate opening – and the fight is a conspicuous example – we find music from Britten that extensively and powerfully embodies the dramatic moment. In the scene of the punch-up between Bunyan and Helson we seem suddenly to be confronted by the composer who, some four years later, was to embark on writing *Peter Grimes* and thus to initiate the long series of works that make him the outstanding musical dramatist of the second half of the twentieth century. (It is an odd thought that the history of Britten as an operatic composer begins, as it were, on – or near – Broadway.) Or to take another example, the very last scene of the work, the Christmas Party, for which Britten writes the longest stretch of continuous music in the whole operetta. It is a genuine finale which also allows for effective recapitulation: the Western Union messenger boy who rides in on his bicycle bearing tidings of Inkslinger's summons to Hollywood does so to the very same music that accompanied the boy's entrance in Act One. It is a show-stopping moment, as is the miniature madrigal or epithalamium which celebrates the forthcoming nuptials of Tiny and Slim and prompted Auden to verses that magically combine the droll with grace and tenderness:

> Put a gold ring on her finger,
>   Press her close to your heart
> While the fish in the lake their snapshots take
>   And the frog, that sanguine singer,
> Sings agreeably, agreeably, agreeably of love.

Vintage Auden!
 Thus the Christmas Party ties all the threads together – Love, the Hollywood Dream, the Cultivation of the Land (the farmer, John Shears, is among the guests) and Public Service:

> And Hel . . .

> Will soon be gone to Washington
>   To join the Administration
> As a leading man in the Federal Plan
>   Of public works for the nation.

That last utterance is unforgettably stamped by the ethic of the WPA and Federal Theater, though in 1941 it was something of a last gasp: the ideals and aspirations of the Roosevelt years were fast fading.

While the placing and continuity of the Christmas Party show a concern for musico-dramatic architecture that was more common in the opera house than on Broadway, Auden and Britten by no means abandoned in their finale the simple and direct style that characterizes *Paul Bunyan* as a whole. It is only perhaps in the very last number of all, the magnificent Litany, that the work seems quite consciously to sever connections with the genre of witty, wise, socially minded entertainment:

> The echoing axe shall be heard no more
> Nor the rising scream of the buzzer saw
> Nor the crash as the ice-jam explodes in the thaw.

> . . .

> No longer the logger shall hear in the Fall
> The pine and the spruce and the sycamore call.

The urgency and passion of the B flat minor on which the Litany is launched scarcely provides the standard happy ending to an evening's entertainment, though of course it prepares one for the solemnities of Bunyan's final rhetoric:

> Where the night becomes the day,
> Where the dream becomes the fact,
> I am the Eternal Guest,
> I am Way,
> I am Act.

The abrupt switch from Christmas jollities to sombre reflection and questioning is perhaps the clearest instance of poet and composer bending the convention of the musical to their own high and individual purposes and, in doing so, transcending and transforming the convention: no one could have expected the chill wind of the Litany to blow the ashes of an extinct campfire across the Christmas decorations.

Milton Smith, the stage director of the original production, remembered his 'attempts to get Auden to do something to give us a more rousing, patriotic *end*', to which Auden replied, 'I don't want to sound like John Latouche'. (John Latouche (1917–56) wrote the words of *Ballad for Americans*, 'a statement of democracy' for voice and orchestra by Earl Robinson (b.1910), first introduced in 1939 in the WPA (Works Progress Administration) production *Sing for Your Supper* and then broadcast on 5 November 1939 with Paul Robeson as soloist. It then, in J. T. Howard's words, 'brought such a deluge of fan mail that it continued its career in movies, on phonograph records, and on symphony orchestra programs . . . It was first heard at a time when Americans were increasingly conscious of the blessings of democracy, and it became one of our most widely used patriotic concert pieces during World War II.' All this no doubt explains Auden's anxiety to avoid sounding like Latouche. Robinson, who studied composition with Copland and Hanns Eisler, was active in the Federal Theater, and in New York in the thirties was a member of the Workers Laboratory Theater and the Composers Collective of the Pierre Degeyter Club. Latouche, a key figure in the Federal Theater/Broadway link-up, was to make his name on Broadway with *Cabin in the Sky* (Vernon Duke, October 1940) and had earlier contributed to *Pins and Needles*, presented by and for members of the International Ladies Garment Workers Union (Harold Rome, 1937, and still running in 1939). He was later to write the libretto for Douglas Moore's folk opera, *The Ballad of Baby Doe* (see also pp. 128 and 135).)

In dwelling on the seriousness of the Litany, I do not want to suggest that the character of *Paul Bunyan* has undergone a comprehensive modification by the time we reach the end of

·he work. The Litany certainly poses a question, which is all the more telling because of what has preceded it. But *Bunyan* successfully maintains for its larger part the exuberance and direct indigenous appeal that were its ambitions, and nowhere more so – or more startlingly – than in the three Ballad Interludes for the Narrator, which, in Auden's own words, were designed to function 'as solo Greek chorus'. This is perhaps not precisely the description that flies to our lips when we hear, after the Prologue, the First Ballad Interlude, which plunges us into the most intensive use of the vernacular to be found anywhere in the work. For these three Ballads, in which the singer accompanies himself on a guitar with a quasi-improvised support of whatever other appropriate instruments happen to be handy, brilliantly and authentically exploit the hillbilly idiom which in later decades has furnished the repertories of various categories of the combined folk and popular style, e.g. blue grass and Country and Western. Once again, Britten has the accent mysteriously at his command. It is extremely difficult to believe that these haunting, folk-like tunes, instinctively American, were imagined by a young English composer only recently out of London and Lowestoft. The Ballads, without doubt, are yet another example of the quickness, accuracy and receptivity of Britten's ear. He could assimilate, and then replicate, the characteristics of a music – and a culture – other than his own perhaps more rapidly than any other comparable composer of his generation. (At an altogether different and more profound level, he was to do exactly the same many years later when, during the briefest of visits to Japan in 1956, he assembled a repertory of characteristic features drawn from Japanese traditional music and put them to use in *Curlew River* in 1964. One could hardly think of two works more strongly contrasted than *Bunyan* and *Curlew River* but the principle involved is precisely the same.)

The context of Auden's reference to the function of the Ballad Interludes was his introductory account of *Paul Bunyan* which appeared in the *New York Times* on 4 May 1941, the day

before the first performance, and which I reproduce on pp. 1
4. What he wrote there – ' . . . the theatrical presentation of
the majority of Bunyan's exploits would require the resources
of Bayreuth, but not to refer to them at all would leave his
character all too vaguely in the air. To get round this difficulty
we have interposed simple narrative ballads between the
scenes, as it were, as solo Greek chorus' – gives the impres-
sion that the Ballads were fundamental to the conception of
the operetta, and perhaps they were; in which case one
wonders how so novel an idea came to the composer and
librettist whose experience of the American scene, when all is
said and done, was relatively limited.

It is in this connection that one recalls an historic chance
encounter between Britten and Kurt Weill which took place in
August 1940, when work on *Paul Bunyan* may have been
suspended but certainly had not been lost sight of. The two
men met while staying at the Owl's Head Inn, Owl's Head,
Maine. 'As you see,' Britten wrote back to Elizabeth Mayer in
Amityville,

> we are still here – & as a matter of fact we have had some
> acquaintance up here. We came into dinner the other
> evening & heard some pretty sophisticated talk going on
> & recognized Kurt Weill! He was spending a few days
> here with Mr. & Mrs. Maxwell Anderson . . . We saw
> quite a lot of him & he really was awfully nice and
> sympathetic, & it was remarkable how many friends we
> had in common, both in Europe & here.

A few days later Britten was writing to one of those old
friends, Gustel, the wife of the conductor Hermann Scher-
chen:

> . . . who should arrive at the same little Inn, miles away
> from anywhere, but Kurt Weill. Naturally we had long
> talks about you & the old days. He is such a nice man.

It is clear that Weill and Britten on this one recorded occasion of a personal meeting got on well; and if there were no more to be said than that, it would still remain a highly interesting fact. But a little further thought gives rise to some illuminating parallels and speculation.

For a start, another common friend was the publisher Hans W. Heinsheimer, who was now working for Britten's publishers in New York and had himself played a leading role in Weill's musical affairs as *his* publisher in Europe in the 1930s. It was Heinsheimer, moreover, who had suggested in the first instance to Britten that he and his poet friend should write a work for the American 'high school', i.e. a theatre piece that would have an educative mission as well as, no doubt, helping to establish themselves as a creative presence on the East Coast. On 29 June 1939, shortly after his arrival in New York from Canada, Britten had written to Ralph Hawkes in London: 'I've seen Heinsheimer & had long talks with him. He has told me that the opportunities are immense . . . for an operetta for children (for which I also have ideas & will write to Wystan Auden).' In making this suggestion Heinsheimer was surely guided by his earlier experience in Europe of socially conscious music theatre, a field in which Weill had proved so brilliantly innovative and successful. It was a tradition that, one might argue, was sustained in the public policies of the Roosevelt government regarding the arts and artists and their relation to a function within the community, and made manifest in Federal concepts like the Works Progress Administration and Federal Theater. Furthermore, Britten and Weill shared at least to some degree a common ambition (which was also no doubt Heinsheimer's). Weill, of course, had been active in the States since 1935; and it had been part of his programme to shake off his European associations and master the musical language of his adopted land, and more particularly the traditions of the American popular theatre. Britten had no conscious intent, I am sure, to sever his links with Europe: after all, his personal history, if

not his politics, had been quite different from Weill's. B
likewise it was his ambition to establish himself as a presence
on the American scene and to do so by means of a work that
was overtly American in character and gesture; and he chose
to do so by attaching himself to the tradition of the 'musical',
to which Weill had already made notable contributions.

At the time of their meeting at the Owl's Head Inn, Weill
was completing the score of *Lady in the Dark* (with a book by
Moss Hart and lyrics by Ira Gershwin). It is amusing in
retrospect to find that the fourth and last of the musical 'dream
sequences' that Weill composed was entitled 'Hollywood
Dream'. Although it never got beyond drafting, because the
show threatened to be overlong, it was (according to David
Drew) composed in the manner of a large-scale operetta
finale, as were the three preceding 'Dreams'. Britten, of
course, was not following Weill's example by intending to
include in *Paul Bunyan*, as finale to Act One, a Lullaby of
Dream Shadows (Film Stars and Models), though as it turned
out this scene was cut just before the first run of performances
in 1941 (see p. 141–4 below), and he showed no inclination to
revive it when revising *Bunyan* in 1974. Both composers,
however, were surely responding to what was an essential,
inescapable fact: that part of the American Dream was the
dreamworld of Hollywood. For Inkslinger, in *Bunyan*, the
dream was to come true:

WESTERN UNION BOY
A telegram, a telegram,
    A telegram from Hollywood.
Inkslinger is the name;
    And I think that the news is good.

INKSLINGER: (*Reading*) 'Technical Adviser required for all-
    star lumber picture stop your name suggested stop if
    interested wire collect stop.'

INKSLINGER
A lucky break, am I awake?
Please pinch me if I'm sleeping.
It only shows that no one knows
The future of bookkeeping.

We have no scrap of evidence to suggest what Weill and Britten may have talked about, though it is difficult to imagine that Britten, on meeting a composer already celebrated for his work in the musical theatre, would not have let drop that he was launching out on a theatre piece of his own. All else must be speculation, but there are at least two points, one minor, one of possibly greater significance, which are worth spelling out. First, in his letter of 19 October 1939 to Ralph Hawkes from which I have already quoted above, Britten specifically mentions the conjunction of a 'professional Broadway performance by the well-known Ballet Caravan'. This thought must have been floated by Heinsheimer, who in turn would certainly have known of the great success scored by Weill just a few months earlier with *Railroads on Parade*, given at the 1939 World's Fair with members of the WPA Theater Project, Ballet Caravan, and the Ted Shawn Dance Company. (The American Ballet Caravan was not to be involved in the first production of *Bunyan*, but later, through his acquaintance with Lincoln Kirstein, Britten was invited to compose his *Matinées Musicales*, Op. 24, for the company, which later became the American Ballet Company.)

The second point is yet more intriguing. In the first months of 1938, Weill himself had contemplated a musical on a specifically American theme, very much of a like character to the folk story of Paul Bunyan. This was *Davy Crockett*, an unfinished project for the Federal Theater, a musical play by H. R. Hays and Kurt Weill. A feature of the score was four so-called Interscenes, which comprised a hillbilly narrative song: all four, according to Drew, were based on the same tune, Josh Hawkins's 'I'm a rolling stone'. Thus one of the most striking

features of *Bunyan* was already adumbrated in Weill's incom-
plete *Crockett* of 1938. The parallel was probably wholly
coincidental, though I suppose there is an outside chance that
the two composers may have found themselves talking about
how most effectively to exploit an authentically American
idiom in their 'American' music. But in any event, whether the
idea was touched on or not, it remains of exceptional interest
that both Weill and Britten utilized the same means not only as
guarantor of atmosphere, but also as embodiment of the
narrative. One notes that Weill's second Interscene ballad told
the tale of Davy Crockett's marriage to Sarah. The Second
Ballad in *Bunyan* performs a similar service with regard to
Paul's marriage to Carrie.

However true to type the melodies of Britten's Ballads may
be, Auden's texts plunder a vocabulary and range of imagery
– and, typically, information – with a dexterity and complica-
tion that were certainly not commonly encountered in hillbilly
songs. There are some inimitably Audenesque things here, in
the Second Ballad, for example, where we hear of Bunyan
recounting his dreams to his lumbermen:

> His phrases rolled like waves on a beach
> And during the course of a single speech
>
> Young boys grew up and needed a shave,
> Old men got worried they'd be late for the grave.

Or, from the Third Ballad:

> Shoulder your axe and leave this place:
> Let the clerk move in with his well-washed face.
>
> Let the architect with his sober plan
> Build a residence for the average man;

> And garden birds not bat an eye
> When locomotives whistle by;
>
> And telephone wires go from town to town
> For lovers to whisper sweet nothings down.

It is in the same Ballad that Auden shows off his topographical knowledge with characteristic bravura (perhaps this is an example of the know-all, too-clever-by-half impression that contributed to the resistances *Bunyan* met on its first performance):

> All over the States the stories spread
> Of Bunyan's camp and the life they led.
>
> Of fights with Indians, of shooting matches,
> Of monster bears and salmon catches.
>
> Of the whirling whimpus Paul fought and killed,
> Of the Buttermilk Line that he had to build.
>
> And a hundred other tales were known
> From Nantucket Island to Oregon.
>
> From the Yiddish Alps to the Rio Grande,
> From the Dust Bowl down to the Cotton Land.

And so on: brilliant and seethingly fertile texts in a ballad vein that in any case came easily to Auden.

The tunes, we may guess, came no less easily to Britten. Indeed, if we turn to the testimony of members of the first cast, among them the original ballad singer, Mordecai Baumann, who was designated 'Narrator' in the 1941 programme, the famous Interludes were very much a last-minute improvisation (as spontaneous, in fact, as they continue to sound). I questioned Baumann about the Ballads in April 1977 in New York:

DONALD MITCHELL: Do you remember anything in particular about the Ballads, or how they were given to you by the composer?

MORDECAI BAUMANN: I remember a lot about it because the words had been written by the time the score had been finished, but none of the music had been put down, and as it got closer and closer to the performance, Milton Smith kept saying, 'Well, what about the music for the narrator? Because we want to tie the piece together through narration.' The reason that the narrator was brought in I imagine was because nothing was happening on stage except ideas. Auden's poetry is beautiful, some of it he even used in his collections of poetry, even though he didn't say it was from *Paul Bunyan*. And the problem for the production was that it's very hard to fly geese in – and land on a lake! – but what happened finally was that one day Britten and Auden and Pears said, 'Look, we got to get that music done for the Ballads' and 'Come on over to Brooklyn.' And they were living in a house in Brooklyn Heights . . .

DM: 7 Middagh Street . . .

MB: Yes . . . and I went over one day and Britten sat down at the piano and he knocked out a lead-sheet for these songs.

DM: Just on the spot?

MB: On the spot, pretty much on the spot. He may have thought about it before, but as far as I know he just wrote it out as I sang it there and that was it. And I brought it back and they didn't even have an accompaniment for it, so I found a guy who played a guitar in the company and a fella who played the double-bass and I said, 'That's my orchestra', and we

THE COLUMBIA THEATER ASSOCIATES

OF COLUMBIA UNIVERSITY

present

PAUL BUNYAN

by W. H. Auden and Benjamin Britten

WITH THE CO-OPERATION OF

The Columbia University Department of Music

AND A CHORUS FROM

The New York Schola Cantorum

Hugh Ross, Conductor

BRANDER MATTHEWS HALL

WEEK OF MAY 5, 1941

Three pages from the original programme, 5 May 1941

PAUL BUNYAN

Book by W. H. Auden; Music by Benjamin Britten

Directed by Milton Smith; Musical Director — Hugh Ross

CHARACTERS

In the Prologue

Old Trees	CHORUS
Young Trees	ELLEN HUFFMASTER, JANE WEAVER, MARLOWE JONES, BEN CARPENS
Three Wild Geese	HARRIET GREENE, AUGUSTA DORN, PAULINE KLEINHESSELINK

In the Interludes

Narrator	MORDECAI BAUMAN

In the Play

The Voice of Paul Bunyan	. MILTON WARCHOFF
Cross Crosshaulson	. WALTER GRAF
John Shears	. LEONARD STOCKER
Sam Sharkey	. CLIFFORD JACKSON
Ben Benny	. EUGENE BONHAM
Jen Jenson	. ERNEST HOLCOMBE
Pete Peterson	. LEWIS PIERCE
Andy Anderson	. BEN CARPENS
Other Lumberjacks . . . . ALAN ADAIR, ELMER BARBER, ARNOLD JAFFE, MARLOWE JONES, CHARLES SNITOW, ROBERT ZELLER, W. FREDRIC PLETTE, THOMAS FLYNN, JOSEPH HARROW	
Western Union Boy	HENRY BAUMAN
Hel Helsen	. BLISS WOODWARD
Johnny Inkslinger	. WILLIAM HESS
Fido	PAULINE KLEINHESSELINK
Moppet	HARRIET GREENE
Poppet	AUGUSTA DORN
The Defeated . . . . BEN CARPENS, EUGENE BONHAM, ADELAIDE VAN WEY, ERNEST HOLCOMBE	

PRODUCTION STAFF FOR "PAUL BUNYAN"

Company Manager . . . . LOREN CROSTEN

Assistant Directors . . . . . ROBERT VAMBERY, LOUISE GIFFORD

Stage Manager . . . . VICTOR KOMOW

Assistant Stage Managers . . . . . . GRETCHEN BURKHALTER
W. FREDRIC PLETTE
THOMAS FLYNN

Property Manager . . . . HARRIET WITTSTEIN

Assistant Property Managers . . . . . RUTHANN SAMPSON
ROSE SLATER

Sound Technician . . . . PROSPER INVERNIZZI

Electrician . . . . STUART MACHLIN

House Manager . . . . H. HOLT RIDDLEBERGER

COLUMBIA THEATER ASSOCIATES
EXECUTIVE COMMITTEE
Milton Smith, Chairman

For The Morningside Players

EDWIN S. FULCOMER
HATCHER HUGHES
MARY LOU PLUGGE
BLISS WOODWARD

For The Columbia College
Players

BRUCE CARTER
EVALD GASSTROM
BENJAMIN HUBBARD
JACK ROSEN

For The Columbia Laboratory
Players

HAROLD CLAUSEN
GERTRUDE KELLER
EDWARD MAMMEN

For The Julliard Institute Opera
Players

LUCIA DUNHAM
CHARLES RASELY
MILTON WARCHOFF

forgot about the orchestra in the pit because that [the Ballad] was not accompanied by the orchestra, and they came on stage with me and they were background and we were kind of a country band and I was the country singer.

DM: In 1941 that was really extraordinary, this kind of folk style . . .

MB: It was a folk style and nobody knew about folk style at that time, and as a matter of fact it turned out to be a very amusing part of the show as I came out . . . between the acts the audience applauded before I began to sing because they had enjoyed the narration and they enjoyed the poetry of it. It was very funny and very humorous and very delightful. And of course I had a great time doing it.

Mordecai Baumann's account of how the narrative interludes were finally sparked into life puts an amusing gloss on the more sober explanation of the Ballads which appears in Auden's introductory article. Solo Greek chorus? Perhaps Auden after all had his tongue in his cheek.

These recollections leave us in no doubt that there was a strong ingredient of the haphazard in the assembling of *Paul Bunyan*. It shows up again in the inconsistencies of the authors' descriptions. What kind of work, one wonders, did they really have in mind? At the very outset there was mention of 'an operetta for children' (June 1939). By October what was proposed was an 'Opera . . . for Broadway', but in the same month (same day!) it was also referred to as a 'school operetta', though with a Broadway production in mind. In November and December, 'opera', 'school operetta' and 'operetta' surface as virtually interchangeable references in Britten's correspondence. (The news had travelled fast. Already on 1 November Humphrey Searle was reporting from London in a New York quarterly (*Modern Music*), ' . . . in

America . . . Britten is writing some [*sic*] high school operas with W. H. Auden.') By the time the first performance was approaching, *Bunyan* was most often referred to as 'opera' without qualification, as for example in a letter Britten wrote to Peggy, the wife of the virtuoso Spanish violinist, Antonio Brosa, on 24 February 1941: 'Life is just one hectic rush at the moment – I have a final playthrough of the opera on Wednesday evening to the cast and there are still *four* complete numbers to be written – .' But on the occasion of the première, no formal designation of the work appeared on the programme: '*Paul Bunyan*, Book by W. H. Auden; Music by Benjamin Britten' was the quasi-Broadway format adopted. On the other hand, in the short descriptive note that formed part of the programme, written by Milton Smith and clearly derived from information supplied by Britten and Auden, we learn that the authors' conception was of a 'choral operetta, " . . . with many small parts rather than a few star roles" '. (To complete the tally, in 1976 when Britten came to authorize the first European radio and stage performances, he settled for 'An operetta in two acts and a prologue' as the definitive version of the work's designation.)

'Choral operetta': that, as we have seen, was a formulation that belonged to the work when it was first performed. Its origins, I believe, must have been rooted in the authors' earliest ideas about *Bunyan*, when it was destined for *school* – American high school – performance. Capable choirs would have been easier to find in high schools and colleges in the thirties than capable soloists; moreover, the very theme of the operetta, its dramatic character, called more for 'collective' than 'individual' expression. Hence the predominance of choral numbers, of which the Prologue is an astonishing example. It reveals unmistakably a mastery and brilliance of choral writing, of the use of the chorus as protagonist, as dramatic agent, which prepares the way for the 'collective' choruses of *Peter Grimes*. The authors themselves, as the programme note emphasizes, downgrade the importance of the solo number: this was to be a work without 'star roles'. There are, in fact, only three solos proper in the whole of *Paul Bunyan*, in the sense of independent numbers that also function as revelations or disclosures of character and/or motive (I exclude the three Ballads, the Western Union Boy's song and Inkslinger's miniature – and exquisite – song of regret (No. 16), which forms a pendant to his aria (No. 14)). These are: Slim's Song (No. 12a); Inkslinger's Song (No. 14); and Tiny's Song (No. 15a).

Inkslinger's number precisely fulfils Auden's concept of him as 'the man of speculative and critical intelligence'. His text is appropriately and amusingly wide-ranging in its literary and cultural references while at the same time it does not omit to recognize that it is those who do manual work who make 'the life of thought possible'. It is through his stomach, Auden tells us, that Johnny learns an essential lesson from his relationship with Paul – hence the plangent refrain of his song: 'But I guess that a guy gotta eat'. For his part, Britten found a music for Inkslinger which, in wonderfully lucid instrumental textures, humanizes the bookkeeper's intellectual speculations and gives him a profile – and a conscience. His song is indubitably the most serious and developed of the solo numbers, and also one of the most extraordinary in its orchestral constitution. *Bunyan* in general is remarkable for the diversity of its orchestral accompaniments, with the composition of the orchestra changing virtually from number to number. Inkslinger's Song is typical: *no* strings (which is often the case in the operetta), woodwind, brass, timpani, xylophone and celesta. It is an arresting combination, the colours and transparency of which perhaps reflect not only the 'intellectual' Johnny (his tiny 'Regret' is scored for woodwind trio!) but also a practical consideration that may have been bound up with the work's inception as a 'school opera'. Britten would certainly have been aware of the strength of the American windband tradition in schools and colleges, and aware too of their prowess. String playing on the other hand was not an integral part of the broad educational scene in the States and Britten clearly kept in mind where the principal skills were to be found among his potential young performers (a point also made by Wilfrid Mellers). This may explain the innovative emphasis given to the wind and percussion in the score of *Bunyan*. For whatever reason Britten alighted on his novel sonorities in 1941,* *Bunyan* set precedents in instrumentation which were to prove highly influential when he came to undertake his ensuing operas.

The 'human type' offering the strongest contrast to Inkslinger is Hel Helson, 'the man of brawns but no brains, invaluable as long as he has somebody to give him orders whom he trusts, but dangerous when his consciousness of lacking intelligence turns into suspicion and hatred of those who possess it'. He has no aria proper – logically, one supposes, because he has no interior life and no dynamic but that of the fist. He is shown instead (in No. 20, 'The Mocking of Hel Helson') putting his slogan-like estimates of himself – Helson the Brave, the Fair, the Wise, the Strong, and so forth – to the sounding-board of animate and inanimate Nature. The answers he receives to his questioning refrain are not the ones he wants to hear; and the outcome of this unsatisfactory debate is 'The Fight' (No. 23) – 'Helson is tough! But Paul has the brains' – in which he receives his comeuppance from Bunyan and finally achieves a limited degree of self-illumination.

Helson is not the stuff of which elaborate arias are made. Nor is Slim, the cowboy, whose song so ingeniously exploits the genre of extrovert, prairie-land music without too much extension of its boundaries.

As for Tiny's solo number, Helen Marshall remembered in 1977 how the song came to be written:

---

*In January 1940, he had visited Champaign, Illinois, where 'I heard lots of wind-bands & met conductors'. It was not until April 1941 that he was working full out on scoring the operetta.

HELEN MARSHALL: Yes, I was the original Tiny. And the only recollection that I have is that I had been singing in a madrigal group with Peter Pears and when he found out that Dr Smith had cast me in the show he evidently said something to Ben about the fact that I could sing a little bit and so, the first time I met Ben, he said, 'Please Helen, what is your range?' So I told him what my vocal range was and the next night he had the Mother aria written for me. It was not in the original score . . .

DM: The amazing speed with which this piece was composed . . .

HM: Just overnight.

And Milton Smith, who was present at this same 1977 interview, added:

> In the original version [of the operetta], although it called for a soprano lead singer, she had nothing to sing but chorus, and the same, there was a tenor who had nothing to sing except in the choruses, and I insisted that each of them had to have something to sing so the boys [Britten and Auden] obliged.

These vivid memories of the original cast were recollected some thirty-six years after the first performance and it could well be that an occasional detail may prove to need correction, though not, I think, Helen Marshall's memory, for the typescript of the libretto clearly shows in Britten's hand the interpolation of Tiny's Song and the lines of text (in Auden's hand) required to introduce the new number (see illustration, p. 124). But it is clear, I think, that the *ad hoc* assembly of some of the solo numbers shows how, as a result of a variety of pressures, practical considerations and seized options, *Paul Bunyan* developed away from its original choral, collective conception and significantly shifted in the direction of

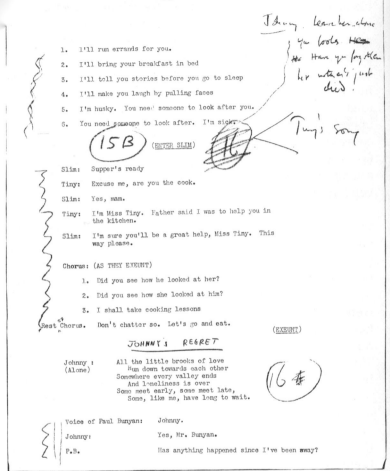

1. I'll run errands for you.

2. I'll bring your breakfast in bed

3. I'll tell you stories before you go to sleep

4. I'll make you laugh by pulling faces

5. I'm husky. You need someone to look after you.

6. You need someone to look after. I'm sick.

(15B) (ENTER SLIM)

Johnny. Leave her alone
You looks
Have you forgotten
her mother's just died!

Tiny's Song

Slim: Supper's ready

Tiny: Excuse me, are you the cook.

Slim: Yes, mam.

Tiny: I'm Miss Tiny. Father said I was to help you in the kitchen.

Slim: I'm sure you'll be a great help, Miss Tiny. This way please.

Chorus: (AS THEY EXEUNT)

1. Did you see how he looked at her?

2. Did you see how she looked at him?

3. I shall take cooking lessons

Rest of Chorus. Don't chatter so. Let's go and eat.

(EXEUNT)

JOHNNY'S REGRET

Johnny :   All the little brooks of love
(Alone)   Run down towards each other
              Somewhere every valley ends
                And loneliness is over
              Some meet early, some meet late,
                Some, like me, have long to wait.

(16#)

Voice of Paul Bunyan: Johnny.

Johnny: Yes, Mr. Bunyan.

P.B.   Has anything happened since I've been away?

A page from the typescript of the original libretto. It shows, in Auden's hand, the additional dialogue required to introduce the last-minute interpolation of Tiny's Song, marked up in Britten's hand

operetta, with its clear distinction between choruses, ens
bles and arias. It was the solo numbers, I think – at least one
which, Tiny's Song, as we have seen, was the result of happy
accident rather than design – which presented the biggest
problem in terms of sequence and location. In short, where
best to place them? This is a complex issue, with a complex,
fluctuating history attached to it, and at least five stages can be
identified in the ordering of the numbers throughout the
operetta: (1) as first composed; (2) possible reordering dis-
cussed *pre*-performance; (3) as established during the first run;
(4) possible revisions contemplated *post*-performance; (5) as
established in the 1974 revised and eventually published
version.

The changing fortunes of Inkslinger's Song, which is
perhaps the nearest thing to an aria proper to show up,
illustrates my point. In the 1941 performance, the song
(No. 14) was heard after the Exit of Lumberjacks (No. 8b) and
near to the end of scene 1 of Act One, with the curious result
that the song and its pendant, Inkslinger's Regret (No. 16),
were split across two scenes, when they should obviously
have been close neighbours. The remaining principal solo
numbers, Slim's Song (No. 12a) – another late addition – and
Tiny's Song (No. 15a), were heard in 1941 where they are
heard today, though Helson's number (No. 20) – in its original
format, of course – was located between Nos. 22 and 23.

I am not at all of the mind that the operetta was – or is –
without dramatic momentum or coherence. But undoubtedly
the peculiar type of narrative it offers – a mix of epic myth and
homely folk tale – and its initial concept, which emphasized
the collective rather than the individual, conspired to make it
difficult to allot a consistent role to the traditional solo. The
most interesting aspect of the 1941 location of Inkslinger's
Song was its departure from the sequence in which *Bunyan*
was composed. In other words, it was a production decision –
an attempt perhaps to space out the solo numbers on a more
even basis throughout the work.

o less interesting, when Britten came to revise *Bunyan* in 74 he returned to the sequence of numbers *as composed* not as irst performed, which meant, among other restorations, that Inkslinger's Song and his Regret were reunited. It also meant, on a broader view, that all the principal solos were now gathered together in a relatively narrow space, not so much strung out as corralled in, as my outline shows:

Solos	*Entrances and Exits*
No. 12a Slim's Song	
	No. 13 Bunyan's Return
No. 14 Inkslinger's Song	
	No. 14a Entrance of Chorus
	No. 15 Tiny's Entrance
No. 15a Tiny's Song	
No. 16 Inkslinger's Regret	
	No. 17 Bunyan's Goodnight (iii)

In 1941, moreover, the column of solos would have been even further strengthened by the addition of Inkslinger's Love Song, which fell by the wayside in 1974.

There is no denying that the order *as composed* (and as restored in 1974) had its own symmetry and logic about it, even though it is understandable that the authors for the production tried to achieve a more conventional alternation of choruses, ensembles and arias. But the fact that the attempt was made is indicative of the diverse formal pressures brought to bear by changing emphases in the operetta's constitution.

Unlike Inkslinger's 'interior' solo, Tiny's Song – her 'Mother' aria – belongs in style above all to the genre of the musical. It was as close as Britten was ever to get to composing a genuine popular song, one that was genuinely rather than artificially sentimental: there's a big difference.

The difference shows up not only in the text (see p. 99

126

above) but also in the music, where Britten, even thou[g]
operating at a distance from what one would have thought t
be his natural self (or at least the self with which we became
familiar from 1942 onwards), none the less remained entirely
true to his own musical chemistry. It is no accident that what
helps Tiny's little song to discriminate between sentiment and
sentimentality is that characteristic Britten device of the
Lydian sharp fourth, common to Tiny's pop song and the
third of the *Michelangelo Sonnets* which had been composed in
1940 (Sonnet XXX: same key!).

Tiny's Song would not only have added substance to the
characterization of Slim's sweetheart but also, and perhaps
more importantly, brought extra relief to the otherwise pre-
dominantly male-voice constitution of the operetta. Auden
and Britten realized that they had landed themselves with a
challenge by choosing a myth that entailed an almost exclusi-
vely male cast, for which reason, as Auden himself (in his *New
York Times* article) remarked, the camp's only genuine camp-
followers – two cats and a dog – were allotted to a trio of
sopranos, one a high soprano, at the furthest extreme from the
baritones and basses of the loggers. Undoubtedly a consider-
ation here was vocal colour (and variety). But for Auden,
animals were a long-standing preoccupation – the world for
him was not mankind alone but 'animals and men', just as the
Litany has it – and indeed possibly the most significant work
of all to result from the Britten–Auden collaboration, the great
orchestral song-cycle from 1936, *Our Hunting Fathers*, had
taken as its theme the relationship of men and animals and
used it, symbolically, to comment on the Nazis' persecution of
the Jews in Europe in the thirties. *Paul Bunyan* did not make
that political point again, but it certainly confirmed in its own
witty manner the importance of animals for the librettist,
which in turn allowed the composer to write two extended
animal numbers, a Trio (No. 8) and Cats' Creed (No. 22), No. 8
accompanied by wind, harp and celesta, No. 22 by woodwind
and a pair of horns, and both of them founts of high colour (in

.ch and intensity), with Fido (the dog), not growling, but elping (a coloratura role).

Tiny's Song, as we have seen, materialized in response to Britten's discovery that Helen Marshall could sing! This reminds me of another factor that was influential in the making of *Paul Bunyan* – the limitations and potentialities of the cast. The concept of communal, workshop theatre was strong at this time, with the implication of opening up the arts to the non-professional. Further – and I am sure this was an additional influence – there was the tradition imported from Europe, in which Weill and Brecht had provided famous precedents, of the actor–singer, a very different being from the straight singer in the musical theatre (or operetta).

There were many considerations and factors, then, that contributed to the evolution and metamorphoses of the operetta; and doubtless yet another influence was the youthful exuberance of its authors, which may have brought in its train some of the consequences of inexperience but added an invigorating dimension of spontaneity, boldness and untrammelled imagination. Something of the irrepressible vitality of the collaboration seems to have marked the very first performance of the work, of which Milton Smith was witness:

MILTON SMITH: The work was composed, and I was asked to go and see in Professor Moore's apartment [Douglas Moore, the composer of *The Devil and Daniel Webster* (1939) and in later years, *The Ballad of Baby Doe* (1956)] three [*sic*] Englishmen who were here who had composed a new American opera. And I went and heard, and I thought the music was so tremendous, so incredibly tremendous that dead or alive I did it.

DM: How did you hear it on that occasion?

MS: I heard the best performance of it that was ever given.

DM: And that was?

MS: Benjamin Britten played the piano, Peter Pears sang all the parts, sang quartets, choruses, duets, whatever you

The original production, Brander Matthews Hall, Columbia University, New York. (i) The Prologue, in which illuminated masks on the trees distinguished Old Trees from Young Trees: behind, the moon that turned blue at Paul Bunyan's birth. (ii) The Camp. Cowboy Slim is centre stage, flanked by the two cats, Moppet and Poppet

have he sang it.

M: Peter sang all that?

MS: Peter. It was a solo performance. Magnificent, incredible, it was the best performance that this opera ever had or will have.

Dr Smith may be forgiven for his numerical slip of the tongue. Pears was not a co-composer but he was very actively involved in the enterprise, not as a singer (except on the occasion to which Milton Smith refers) but as a copyist: many of the manuscript materials held at the Britten–Pears Library at Aldeburgh are in Pears's hand. As it turned out, *Paul Bunyan* was to be the only opera of Britten's in which he did not have a key role, no doubt for the reason that in the context of an all-American opera, an English singer and his English accent (above all in the long stretches of spoken dialogue) would have struck a chronically inauthentic note. However, retrospective justice was done. When the operetta was revived in a BBC studio broadcast in 1976, the role of Johnny Inkslinger was undertaken by Pears (the spoken dialogue throughout the production was delivered by a separate cast of actors).

And how was the first performance – the first performance in the theatre on 5 May 1941 as distinct from the Pears one-man show – received? Olin Downes wrote in the *New York Times* on 6 May 1941, under the headlines 'Official Opening for "Paul Bunyan" – Work Is Called Meritorious – Many of Singers From Amateur Ranks':

Composing Is Adroit

Mr. Britten *had* prepared us for the plausibility and adroitness of his *composing* by symphonic works which have met with a considerable measure of success in concert halls on both sides of the Atlantic. He is a very clever young man, who can provide something [in] any style or taste desired by the patron. He scores with astonishing expertness and fluency. He has a melodic vein which is perfectly plausible, though one without marked physiognomy. He shows what could be done by a composer whose purpose was deeper set and more consistent than Mr. Britten's appears to be. For this reason the respects in which he was lacking were disappointing, at times irritating.

As for Mr. Auden, we had expected better of him. It need not have been anticipated that a modern English poet of his nature and antecedents would impart a very characteristic flavor to an essentially American legend. Nor need it have been expected that a literary man's early venture into the theater would have the salient strokes and developments of stage-craft that would thrust home his interpretation. But we had a right to hope for something from him that would have consistently developed purpose. Whereas his libretto, like the music, seems to wander from one to another idea, without conviction or cohesion. In the plot, as in the score, is a little of everything, a little of symbolism and uplift, a bit of socialism and of modern satire, and gags and jokes of a Hollywood sort, or of rather cheap musical comedy . . .

What is done by Mr. Britten shows more clearly than ever that opera written for a small stage, with relatively modest forces for the presentation, in the English language, and in ways pleasantly free from the stiff tradition of either grand or light opera of the past, is not only a possibility but a development nearly upon us.

The flexibility and modernity of the technical treatment were refreshing. That they are derivative does not alter this salient and striking fact. We do not know whether the authors of this piece are conversant, for example, with the terse and savage social satire of *The Cradle Will Rock* [Marc Blitzstein (1937)], of recent and highly honorable achievement. But it seems likely.

s for the sources of Mr. Britten's style, they are
nerous and extremely eclectic. They range every-
re from Prokoffieff to Mascagni, from Rimsky-Kor-
off to Gilbert and Sullivan. Few operas are neglected
ow of recognition as he proceeds. One would say that
was extremely conversant with the entire repertory of
e lyric theater and that as a modern craftsman he could
ite in any style known to man regardless of period.
He knows how to set a text, how to orchestrate in an
onomical and telling fashion; how to underscore dia-
gue with orchestral commentary, terse or more elabor-
ately descriptive, and how to treat all this with an
ingenuity that only palls when he has exhausted devices
and is faced with the necessity of saying something
genuine. Then the music begins to fail, the set numbers
to become wearisome and the listeners to tire of ingenui-
ties which are seen before the evening is over as plati-
tudes and notion counter devices of salesmanship.

In the *World Telegram* of 5 May, Robert Bagar quotes a new
description of *Paul Bunyan*, 'an *allegorical* operetta based on an
American lumber camp legend' (my italics), and pursued that
theme at the beginning of his notice:

The allegories brushed each other aside in their mad
rush for the spotlight. Paul Bunyan, lumber-jack super-
myth of epic proportions and derring-doodles, received
a few more powers from the bountiful authors He was,
to start with 'a projection of the collective state of mind of
a people whose tasks were primarily the physical mas-
tery of nature'. Then he became Courage, Hope, the
Good Companion, the Present, the Future, the Infinite.
He was all of these, but he couldn't imitate four
Hawaiians.
    In conveying the idea to a rather befuddled public

Messrs. Britten and Auden depended heavily on a conglomerate throng of characters – 'many small parts rather than a few star roles'. Thus, there were singing trees, singing geese, singing cats, a singing dog, and many, very many singing people. Most of these talked, too . . .

Mr. Britten, who is an up and coming composer, has written some worth-while tunes in this score. It ranges, in passing, from part writing to single [simple] jingle. Its rhythms are often interesting and the harmonies fit rather well. There are arias, recitatives, small ensembles and big choral sequences. Most of the last named are good. The music makes occasional reference to *Cavalleria Rusticana* and one item, a stuttering bit, goes right back to *The Bartered Bride* . . .

Part of the text was clever, part of it literature, but most of it was plain jumble – and 'significant' jumble at that. Of the numbers a Blues, sung by a quartet, The Defeated, proved effective as to both words and music . . .

Bagar's reference to Mascagni (like Downes's) is obscure but he was certainly right in pointing out that John Shears's tongue-tied speech at the Christmas Party had its origins in Smetana. He was also being more prophetic than he could have known at the time: Smetana and John Shears between them were to provide the model for a tongue-locked Albert Herring in 1947.

Britten always remembered the original press reception of *Paul Bunyan* as wholly hostile and adverse, though in fact Olin Downes's account was not without its positive perceptions. Virgil Thomson, on the other hand, in the *New York Herald Tribune* (5 May), was characteristically waspish. The headline was 'Musico-Theatrical Flop', and under it Thomson disposed first of Auden's theatrical manner – 'flaccid and spineless and without energy' – and then of Britten's music:

. . . here as elsewhere, [it] has considerable animation. His style is eclectic though not without savour. Its particular blend of melodic 'appeal' with irresponsible counterpoint and semi-acidulous instrumentation is easily recognizable as that considered by the British Broadcasting Corporation to be at once modernistic and safe. Its real model is, I think, the music of Shostakovitch, also eclectic, but higher in physical energy content than that of Mr. Britten.

Mr. Britten's work in 'Paul Bunyan' is sort of witty at its best. Otherwise it is undistinguished. It is not well written for voices. Neither is it very apt as musical declamation. And the accompaniments tend to obscure rather than to sustain the soloists. Melodically and harmonically it lacks the tension that we recognize as style. There is every reason to suppose Mr. Britten can do better. He usually does.

What any composer thinks he can do with a text like 'Paul Bunyan' is beyond me. It offers no characters and no plot. It is presumably, therefore, an allegory or a morality; and as either it is, I assure you, utterly obscure and tenuous. In addition, its language is not the direct speech of dramatic poetry. It is a deliberate parody, for the most part, of the attempts at intensity on the part of our least dramatic poets. Its subject, consequently, is not Paul Bunyan at all, nor even the loggers and farmers of the Northwest that it purports to depict. Its subject is literature itself, as is that of most of Mr. Auden's work. Every sentence is indirect and therefore unsuited to musical declamation. Every dramatic moment has the afflatus taken out of it before the composer can get it over to the audience . . .

The rendition of the piece was amateurish but not dull. Mr Mordecai Baumann sang nice ditties to a guitar between the scenes. The scenery itself was adequate, if not very interesting. It did its worst at the beginning, where for a full scene and a half the music was choral, the chorus both invisible as to bodies and incomprehensible as to diction. During all this time we watched a dim stage with nobody on it but a couple of ducks and wondered if the show would ever stop talking about itself and get going. Finally some people came out on the stage, and the whole thing lasted till half past eleven; but it never did get going, and I never did figure out the theme . . .

The sense of discouragement engendered by largely adverse criticism may have been real enough at the time – the gloom generated in Britten by temporary setbacks in the past tended to be inflated rather than diminished by memory – but it was not so severe as to prevent him and his collaborator planning a revised version of the operetta. For example, Britten wrote to Douglas Moore from California on 24 June 1941 after the first series of performances to thank him for his support and encouragement and added:

> You may be interested to know that the old piece is now undergoing thorough revision which I shall be delighted to show you when I return to New York in the Fall. Apparently the wreck is worth salvaging because in spite of the bangs it received there is genuine interest being shown in it in various quarters.

He made the same point in a slightly earlier letter (12 May) to his sister Beth, which also perhaps best sums up his feelings after the first run was over:

> The opera 'Paul Bunyan' I think you'd like a lot – full of tunes that people even whistle! and it's quite good entertainment – but the labour involved was enormous – a whole evening's work is no joke to write & score, let

alone supervise the rehearsals. The performance wasn't too good, but there are future productions in sight, which may be better.

To embark on a complete account of the contemplated revisions (which Britten and Auden never brought to completion) would occupy an inordinate amount of space. Moreover, an account of these has already been published, in 1985, by J. P. Frayne, to which interested readers may refer, while Edward Mendelson has in hand the critical edition of the libretto, its variants and revisions, as I have mentioned already in my Prefatory Note. But the principal modifications the authors seem to have had in mind can be quite briefly outlined. Their main objective was to try to make the dramatic argument more coherent and explicit, indeed to import into the operetta a clearly spelled-out element of dramatic tension or conflict that reviewers in 1941 had found lacking. Perhaps in another – and mistaken – attempt to respond to their critics they appear to have thought seriously about ridding the operetta of certain numbers which had been assessed as trivial, frivolous or merely eccentric.

The post-first-performance revision reshaped the operetta into a Prologue and four acts (as distinct from the Prologue and two acts of the original version: the Christmas Party was to be the new Act Four), added yet further dialogue and speeches in the interests of dramatic clarification (a dubious exercise), reordered the sequence of certain numbers and, of course, cut others: characters were dropped and their numbers along with them.

It is this last area that causes dismay. To go were the Western Union Boy's Song, the Cooks' Duet, the Animal Trio, the Food Chorus and the second of the Ballad Interludes. This was surely a gross over-reaction to often superficial or simply dim criticism. If carried through it would have led to the loss of a quantity of music and texts which today strike us as among the most original, arresting and entertaining ideas and inspirations that *Paul Bunyan* has to offer. One is grateful that Britten took a different view when making a final revision of the work for the performances broadcast and staged in 1976 and later publication (posthumously) in 1978. His last revisions spanned the years 1973–5, but in the main were concentrated in 1974. Hereafter I shall refer to the '1974 revision' as a means of identifying the composer's final reassessment of his youthful operetta.

The proposed American revisions led nowhere and there were no further performances of *Paul Bunyan* until the last year of Britten's life. What, I think, relegated the operetta to the composer's bottom drawer was not adverse criticism or his rejection of the work and its librettist – Britten was in close and admiring touch with Auden well after the *Bunyan* affair was over, and contemplating a further ambitious collaboration (*For the Time Being*) – but rather, the result of a fundamental change of location and way of life – one might almost say, of culture. The return to England in March 1942 was the critical watershed. Once that line was crossed, the decision taken finally to return *home*, then, for Britten, the American years were over and behind him. Small wonder that the most overtly American of the works belonging to the American period – a bid to make a specifically American contribution to American culture – was stored away and lingered on only as a spectral title in the list of Britten's unpublished compositions. (It took long enough, in all conscience, for other large-scale works from the American years – the Violin Concerto, *Sinfonia da Requiem, Diversions, Scottish Ballad* – to establish themselves in the repertory, even though these did not display markedly American features.)

What were the motives for the resurrection of *Paul Bunyan* in the 1970s? In May 1973 – the year in which Auden was to die, in September – Britten underwent major open-heart surgery in London. The consequences – physical (a slight but disabling stroke during the operation) and psychological – were severe. He found himself unable any longer to play the piano and for a significant period suffered from a composing 'block'. It was in an attempt to break through that obstacle that the idea of a revived *Paul Bunyan* surfaced. Why not persuade the composer to look at this early – and to most of us about him, with the exception of Peter Pears, totally unknown – work, and reconsider the silence that had been imposed on it for some thirty-three years? Perhaps out of the contact with a half-forgotten piece from his youth he might be encouraged into composing again, to acquire again the confidence that he seemed painfully to have lost, along with the use of his right hand. The principal motive, at the time, was therapeutic. (The same strategy led to the revision and publication, in 1975, of the early String Quartet in D, composed in 1931.)

A crucial stage in the process of recovery, Britten's own as well as the reclamation of his operetta, took place at the 1974 Aldeburgh Festival when eight excerpts from *Bunyan*, including (ironically) a significant proportion of the numbers that were up for excision in the 1941 revision, were performed by four voices and piano – Heather Harper, Janet Baker, Peter Pears (Inkslinger) and John Shirley-Quirk, with Steuart Bedford at the piano. Pears, who had given an illustrated talk about the work earlier in the year, at the Royal Society of Arts in London, on 2 May, wrote in the Programme Book:

> Recently, when pressure was brought to bear on Britten to take the score out again in hopes of revising it and using it, he came to the same conclusion as he had thirty-three years ago. But when I saw and heard again some of the songs which I had copied out in those old days, I persuaded the composer to let us sing them, as I knew the original singers had enjoyed them and as I hope today's [23 June] audience will.

This was not the only representation of *Bunyan* at the 1974 Festival. A few days earlier, on 10 June, an audience had heard the Wandsworth School Choir sing the three Ballads, in a version for boys' choir and piano, the piano taking over the role of the guitar, the boys rendering the melodies in unison. Britten took the opportunity to revise the tunes a little and establish a basic accompaniment, which in future performances could form the basis of any appropriate instrumental improvisation.

These events were crucial first steps which finally resulted in Britten's change of mind. In the summer of the same year he spent a few days at my home at Barcombe Mills in Sussex, bringing with him his manuscript full score of the operetta. The weather was clement and we spent a lot of time in the garden, Britten looking through his score and pondering what revisions he would wish to make if a revival of the work were to go ahead.

He still found it difficult to commit himself to a *stage* production, influenced, maybe, even in the seventies by the adverse comments from the forties on the first staging of the work, when so much criticism fastened on the supposed impracticality and ineffectiveness of the dramatic concept. It was for this reason that we came up with the idea of yet another intermediate stage· a *radio* production which would enable Britten to hear the work in its entirety and finally decide whether *Bunyan* should be returned to the bottom drawer or released from captivity.

The revisions Britten made to the score of the operetta in the light of his 1974 reconsideration of it were relatively slender. Perhaps the most interesting aspect of his approach was a pretty clear resolve to stick in most essentials to the shape of the work as he and Auden had originally conceived it. The revisions that had been contemplated in 1941 after the first performances played little part, fortunately, in the reassessment of 1974. Britten, indeed, proved to be fiercely protective of the integrity of his first full-length theatrical work. When a much respected but perhaps rather grand BBC drama producer wanted to impose his own ideas on how *Bunyan* was to be presented for a radio audience, ideas that included some reordering of numbers and the invention, here and there, of a few lines of pastiche Auden, the composer was highly indignant. Another producer was found, who agreed not to meddle, as Britten saw it, with his and Auden's work. If any revising or improving was to be done, that was his affair; and he felt touchingly competent to act on Auden's and his own behalf without outside, 'bossy' advice. It was on this basis that the radio production got back on the rails again. The eventual success of it paved the way for the first European stage performance at the 1976 Aldeburgh Festival, directed by Colin Graham, who had long been an enthusiast for the revival of the operetta.

The 1974 reworkings fall into three clear categories: (a) Additions, (b) Omissions, (c) Revisions of individual numbers. Two numbers entirely fresh to the score are the orchestral Introduction (No. 1) to the Prologue and Bunyan's third Goodnight (No. 17). When the operetta was originally planned, there was to be an extensive orchestral overture preceding the Prologue. The overture is extant in a complete version for two pianos, but whether Britten ever scored it himself or abandoned it in 1941 on the grounds of excessive length, we do not know. No manuscript full score has survived, and when Britten came to his reconsideration of 1974 there was no question of reviving the overture. ('We can't have an overture *and* a prologue before the opera gets going.')*

The new Introduction – Britten clearly felt that something more was required to precede the Prologue than one bar of C major – was twenty-one bars long and shows how skilfully, and with seeming ease, he could think himself back into a musical world he had quitted long ago. Likewise, No. 17, Bunyan's third Goodnight, though here one recognizes the

---

*Colin Matthews was later to score the overture, which was published as an independent item in 1980.

weight of a lifetime's experience – of composing, of life
behind the music that accompanies and matches the magnifi
cent music of Auden's text:

> Now let the complex spirit dissolve in the darkness
> Where the Actual and the Possible are mysteriously
>   exchanged.
> For the saint must descend into Hell; that his order
>   may be tested by its disorder
> The hero return to the humble womb; that his will
>   may be pacified and refreshed.
> Dear children, trust the night and have faith in
>   tomorrow,
> That these hours of ambiguity and indecision may
>   be also the hours of healing.

The passage, so well described by Peter Evans – 'its strained
[bird] calls (high bassoon and bass clarinet) and dark har-
monies painting the mystery of the night with a beauty that is
no less individual for the evident debt to Bartók' – ends on the
repeated and fading call of the whippoorwill, a North Ameri-
can bird of nocturnal habits. It was typical of Britten that he
insisted on finding a nocturnal birdcall proper to the North
American continent for use in his new closing music to Act
One. Much ornithological research went into producing a
precise model birdcall on which Britten was able to base his
own transcription.

This new finale for the close of Act One also involves the
second category of revision, (b) – Omissions. The original end
of Act One was composed as the extended Lullaby of Dream
Shadows, (Film Stars and Models) that I have already men-
tioned (see p.111 above). It followed on directly after Bunyan's
farewell to Johnny Inkslinger, 'Goodnight. Happy dreams.'
And Inkslinger, it seems, was to dream of Hollywood. But
Britten had never been happy with the dream sequence that
ensued and in 1974 deleted it – crossed it out –

Act 4 P.S.

Chorus:
You've no idea how dull it is
Just being perfect nullities,
    The idols of a democratic nation;
The heros of the multitude,
Their dreams of female pulchritude;
    We're VERY VERY tired of admiration.

[~~SONG OF THE VERY VERY SNOBS~~]

(LULLABY AGAIN BUT SUNG OFF BY CHORUS)

new ① (CURTAIN)

Paul Bunyan:

Now let the complex spirit dissolve in
                                                the darkness
Where the Actual and the Possible are mysteriously exchanged
For the saint must descend into Hell; that his order may
                                                be tested by its disorder
The hero returns to the ~~womb~~ humble ~~womb~~ womb; that
                                his will may be purified and refreshed

Dear children, trust the night and have faith in to-morrow
That these hours of ambiguity and indecision may
                                        be also the hours of healing

End of Act I Sc. 2.

The end of Act One in the typescript of Britten's copy of the original libretto. The addition, in Auden's hand, is the revision that was proposed in 1941, for which Britten composed accompanying music in 1974 but retained the text – 'Now let the complex spirit' – which I have just quoted in its entirety. In Britten's copy of the typed libretto, which in all essentials represents the work as it was heard in 1941, the text of Paul Bunyan's concluding speech was added in Auden's hand (see the facsimile on p. 142). It was clearly intended to follow the reprise of the Lullaby. There was no accompanying music written or envisaged – the act was to close with and on Paul's voice alone.

Britten's decision to take out the dream sequence in 1974 meant that he had to plan a new finale. Happily, the right text was to hand, and 'Now let the complex spirit' was marvellously *re*-imagined for voice and orchestra. Thirty-three years on, one may think, Britten, with Auden's inspiration to hand, alighted on the perfect solution to the end of the operetta's first act.

Thus a combination of old text and new music was to replace the abandoned Lullaby of Dream Shadows. Was this finale in fact abandoned *before* the run of performances started or after the show opened? I have mentioned above the private recording of a live performance of *Bunyan* made at some point during the first run. The recording, though an historic document of extraordinary value, is primitive in acoustic quality – the music is sometimes barely audible. But it does enable us to hear – and still enjoy – Mordecai Baumann in the Ballad Interludes and Helen Marshall in her 'Mother' aria.

We do not hear the Lullaby, however, which does not exist on the recording and which we must presume therefore was cut, along – inexplicably – with Bunyan's spoken Goodnight. The result of knocking off the end of Act One was an excursion into Act Two, in search of the first available alternative conclusion. This was provided by the music for the Farmers' Exit (No. 19a) for orchestra alone; and it was this number which in 1941 brought the curtain down after the first act.

There can, in fact, have been little opportunity for advance planning of how to fill the gap created by the excision of the original finale, for I believe there is evidence to show that the

Lullaby *was* probably performed but only on the occasion of the preview performance, which took place on 4 May, the night before the show opened officially. That the Lullaby was part of the production until a very late stage seems to me to be indicated by the appearance of Film Stars and Models in the cast list of the programme, together with the names of the singers undertaking the roles, even though, as it turned out, their scene was to be abolished (there was no time, it is clear, to amend the printed programme). Yet more illuminating, when we read a complete text of Robert Bagar's review of the operetta, parts of which I have quoted above, we find him specifically mentioning as anachronistic the presence of 'two Film Stars and two Models'. And why should he have done that, if they had not been visible – and presumably vocal – on stage? It is the *date* of his notice that clinches the matter – 5 May 1941. For it to appear then, he must have reviewed the preview which took place the night before the première; and indeed when we reach the very last sentence of his long review he obligingly confirms our deduction: 'Last evening's showing was a preview for members of the League of Composers.' Naturally enough when Olin Downes came to write *his* review of the official first performance on the 5th, published on the 6th, he made no mention of Film Stars and Models; and their Lullaby, one must assume, had vanished (literally) overnight.

The metamorphosing of *Bunyan*, it is clear, had by no means ceased even when the production was in full swing, the doubts and debates attended the making of the work up to and beyond its launch in Brander Matthews Hall. The preparations for that were graphically described by Britten in a letter to Albert Goldberg, the State Supervisor of the Illinois Music Project, dated 28 April 1941:

> I'm just in the middle of rehearsals of my 'Paul Bunyan' operetta – &, believe me, compared with conditions there the Works Project Administration of Illinois is a

mixture of the Boston Symphony, the Ritz-Carlton leading hotel] and the Gestapo (for efficiency only!).

I include, as Appendix A, the text of the original finale to Act One, Lullaby of Dream Shadows (Film Stars and Models),* while the facsimile on p. 142 of the typescript of Auden's libretto – the end of the Lullaby – shows the draft of the text which now forms the conclusion of Act One (some additional annotations are in Britten's hand). One must regret the musical loss of the exquisite Lullaby, 'Say O say farewell', but the babble of the models and film stars, which the Lullaby frames, is conspicuously lacking in fizz, and Britten was wise to let the number rest in the oblivion to which it was so suddenly consigned in 1941.

The second omission was that of 'The Love Song', the text of which appears as Appendix B. This number was heard during the first run, but Britten decided that Auden's dazzling word games had not been easily digestible in (or by) music and had not led him to write a song in 1941 that he wanted to live with in 1974. It is possible too that there was something about the song which for Britten in the seventies uncomfortably raised the shades of Gilbert and Sullivan, two potent influences extremely difficult to keep at bay when it came to rapid word-setting and torrential rhyming in the context of musical comedy (the Love Song is not the only number in *Bunyan* when, to English ears at least, Gilbert and Sullivan threaten to break surface).

I have come to regret the exclusion of the song, however, which seems to me to offer a lot of charm and ingenuity and, more importantly, establishes Inkslinger as a kind of talking – no, singing – dictionary. Words for Johnny are very literally *his* food, the stuff of his mental life, and as we have observed, he has to learn from Paul that the other kind of food, which

*In 1980, at the Aldeburgh Festival, the 'Dream Shadows' finale was performed in a version for voices and piano as part of a programme of excerpts from Britten's theatrical music largely from the pre-war period.

...orts life, has to be worked for and paid for. The omission ...is inexhaustible string of synonyms is to deprive him of an ...portant dimension of his character. In the 1941 performance the Love Song was placed between the Entrance of Chorus (No. 14a) and Tiny's Entrance (No. 15).

For the rest, there were no further omissions and the revisions to other numbers (category c) were of a relatively minor order, involving Slim's Song (No. 12a), Tiny's Song (No. 15a) and The Mocking of Hel Helson (No. 20). In this last number, the need for a revision reflected, yet again, the hitherto low profile accorded the solo number. In 1941 it was a *silent* Helson whose mocking was prompted by two questioning sopranos. In 1974 the composer was able to make Helson articulate by giving him what he had not given him in 1941, a vocal profile of his own: i.e. he converted the number as originally conceived into a solo for Helson while retaining the interventions from Nature. Even had this idea occurred to Britten in 1941, he would have found himself landed with the problem of his soloist's capabilities. The rueful recollections in 1977 of the first Hel Helson, Bliss Woodward, make the point:

BLISS WOODWARD: The one thing that stands out in my mind is that after the fight with Paul Bunyan and I'm carried back on unconscious I do remember the anguish that I caused Mr [Hugh] Ross [the conductor] every time I came in with my musical introduction (Fig. 15 + 1), because I'm not a singer! He died a thousand deaths as I became conscious.
DM: How did you get into the show if you weren't a singer?
BW: Well, I was a member of the Morningside Players and the Columbia Theater Associates . . . and I was very active in amateur theatricals.
HELEN MARSHALL: And a very good actor, may I say.

There, in that exchange, we have in a nutshell the actor–singer problem (that other influential bit of the Brecht–Weill

legacy) which added to Britten's difficulties in 1941 – or in t₂
case the problem of the gifted actor who, alas, could not sin₂
but had a leading role all the same.

Britten in 1974 also paid attention to Slim's Song, adding the
realistic touch of the horse's hooves (woodblock). The princi-
pal revision, however, was the mending of a lacklustre middle
section, and if I remember vividly the occasion that he played
the renovated aria through to me, at Chapel House, Horham,
it was because it was the last time I was ever to hear him play
the piano. This was when he was still hoping, by persistence
and finger exercises, to recover the mobility of his right hand,
and I clearly recall how he had to strive to co-ordinate the
melody with the syncopations of the accompaniment. I also
remember, however, that he took pleasure in the freshness
and ingenuity of the number, and smiled when he had done
with it.

The performance for radio, with the help of many sympath-
etic friends and colleagues too numerous to mention here,
was rehearsed, went into the BBC studios (at Manchester),
and recorded. It was among the very last recordings and
performances of his music in which Britten was able to be
involved even though it was only by consultation. When he
came to hear the recording, he was deeply moved by the
operetta he had created with his old friend all those years ago
on Long Island. Auden, in 1976, when the operetta was first
broadcast, was already dead. Ironically, in what must have
been a fiftieth birthday tribute to Britten which was never
completed or published, Auden took most of the blame on
himself for the operetta's 'failure'.* 'I knew nothing whatever
about opera or what is required of a librettist,' he wrote. 'In
consequence, some very lovely music of Britten's went down

---

*However, he collected three texts from the operetta in later editions of his
poetry, 'Gold in the North came the blizzard to say' (the Blues in Act One);
'Carry her over the water' (from the Christmas Party in Act Two); and 'The
single creature leads a partial life' (the Animal Trio in Act One). Full
publication details appear in Bloomfield and Mendelson, p. 253 (K3).

drain, and I must now belatedly make apologies to my old friend, while wishing him a very happy birthday.' Generous words; and perhaps Auden would have been pleased to think that in the very last year of his friend's life, Britten's 'lovely music' made a triumphant return, convincing even the once reluctant composer that he had been right to let the work live again. He was profoundly touched – sometimes to tears – by such things as 'Once in a while the odd thing happens' – 'That was Peter,' he once confided about that particular chorus: it was during the American years, I believe, that they finally decided that they were meant for each other – and the great Litany at the end of Act Two. It was inescapable that Auden's words and his own sombre music –

> The campfire embers are black and cold,
> The banjos are broken, the stories are told,
> The woods are cut down, and the young grown old.

– should have had a special resonance for him. He turned to me on one occasion in the Library at the Red House, Aldeburgh, after listening to a tape of the BBC recording and said, 'You know, Donald, I simply hadn't remembered that it was such a strong piece.' It is a judgement of *Paul Bunyan* that I believe will come to be widely shared in the future.

Acknowledgements and Sources

I gratefully acknowledge the following individuals, institutions and sources of information: The Literary Executor (Edward Mendelson) and Executors of W. H. Auden, for permission to reproduce hitherto unpublished excerpts from the libretto of *Paul Bunyan*; Steuart Bedford; B. C. Bloomfield and Edward Mendelson, *W. H. Auden, A Bibliography*, 1924–1969, Charlottesville, University Press of Virginia, 1972; Britten's correspondence, for permission to quote from which I am indebted to the Trustees of the Britten–Pears Foundation. Further use of these quotations is not to be made without their written permission; Britten's manuscript full score, the manuscript vocal score, which is largely in the hand of Peter Pears, and the composer's copy of the original libretto (typescript and manuscript draft revisions), in the possession of the Britten–Pears Library and Archive at Aldeburgh; David Drew, *Kurt Weill: A Handbook*, London, Faber, 1987; Peter Evans, *The Music of Benjamin Britten*, London, Dent, 1979, pp. 95–103; Faber Music for permission to quote from the published libretto (1976) and published vocal score (1978); J. P. Frayne, '*Paul Bunyan*'s second chances: revisions and revivals', *American Music*, 3/1, Champaign, Spring 1985; J. T. Howard, *Our American Music*, New York, Crowell, 1946, pp. 551–2; Colin Matthews, 'Britten's Indian Summer', *Soundings*, 6, Cardiff, 1977, pp. 42–9; Wilfrid Mellers, '*Paul Bunyan*: The American Eden' in *The Britten Companion*, ed. Christopher Palmer, London, Faber, 1984, pp. 97–103; Edward Mendelson, for much information and many insights; Donald Mitchell and John Evans, *Benjamin Britten: Pictures from a Life, 1913–1976*, London, Faber, 1978; Donald Mitchell, *Britten and Auden in the Thirties*, London, Faber, 1981; Donald Mitchell, 'What do we know about Britten now?' in *The Britten Companion*, op. cit, pp. 39–45; the New York Times Company; Philip Reed; Edward R.

ly; Milton Smith, Hugh Ross and members of the original ₄1 cast of *Paul Bunyan*, interviewed in New York in 1977; Rosamund Strode; Eric Walter White, *Benjamin Britten, His Life and Operas*, London, Faber, 1983, pp. 115–19; Paul Wilson; Philip Winters, private communications; and my wife, Kathleen, and Judy Young who steered my text through almost as many metamorphoses as the operetta.